D0853350

LAUGHING OUT LOUD

AND OTHER RELIGIOUS EXPERIENCES

OTHER BOOKS BY TOM MULLEN:

Mountaintops and Molehills
Seriously, Life is a Laughing Matter
Birthdays, Holidays, and Other Disasters
Parables for Parents and Other Original Sinners
Where 2 or 3 Are Gathered Together, Someone Spills His
     Milk
The Dialogue Gap
The Ghetto of Indifference
The Renewal of the Ministry

TOM MULLEN

LAUGHING OUT LOUD

AND OTHER RELIGIOUS EXPERIENCES

WORD BOOKS
PUBLISHER
WACO, TEXAS

A DIVISION OF
WORD, INCORPORATED

LAUGHING OUT LOUD AND OTHER RELIGIOUS EXPERIENCES

Library of Congress Cataloguing in Publication Data:

   Mullen, Thomas James, 1934–
      Laughing out loud and other religious experiences.
      1. Wit and humor—Religious aspects—Christianity
   I.   Title
   BR115.H84M84   1983   248.4   83-3643
   ISBN 0-8499-0329-7

Printed in the United States of America

All Scripture references, unless otherwise identified, are from the King James Version of the Bible. Quotations marked TEV are from Today's English Version of the Bible, © American Bible Society 1966, 1971, 1976. Quotations marked RSV are from the Revised Standard Version of the Bible, copyright 1946, 1952, © 1971, 1973 by the Division of Christian Education of the National Council of the Churches of Christ in the U.S.A.

The following copyrighted material is reprinted with permission: "Ode to a Cow" (p. 25), by Arthur Guiterman, copyright 1939, reprinted by permission of Louise H. Sclove. "The Cow" (p. 26), copyright 1931 by Ogden Nash. First appeared in *The New Yorker*. Cartoon by Clayton D. Powers (p. 48), reprinted from *Esquire* (December 1965). Copyright © 1965 by Esquire Associates. "Unspoken War Prayer" (p. 62), abridged excerpt in "The War Prayer" from EUROPE AND ELSEWHERE by Mark Twain. Copyright 1923, 1951 by the Mark Twain Company. Reprinted by permission of Harper & Row Publishers. Cartoon by Betty Swords (p. 67), copyright R. M. Hurley, *Male Chauvinist Pig Calendar* 1974. Excerpt from Ann Landers syndicated column (p. 100), copyrighted by Field Newspaper Syndicate, date and newspaper unknown.

Once Again, to Nancy

CONTENTS

PREFACE

The purpose of this book is to make people laugh and think about their laughter at the same time. This is not easily done, for nothing kills a joke faster than explaining it.

Even so, herein we are trying to have our cake and eat it, too, no small task for an author who is an insulin-taking diabetic. The original title, *Funny Things Happen on the Way to the Cemetery,* was changed because too many people thought it referred, as one of my colleagues thought, to a collection of stories shared while riding in funeral cars. In fact, it is a metaphor for life, which is full of funny things, even though we all move steadily toward a cemetery. The book argues that a Christian perspective provides ample room for humorous laughter, just as it is well acquainted with grief. Frederick Buechner states it profoundly: "[Laughter] comes from as deep a place as tears come from, and in a way it comes from the same place."

Thus, we hope the book provokes both laughter and reflection. Each chapter has a set of questions to stimulate conversation. The idea is to read the book and discuss it as a group. Doing this will probably help readers gain additional insights the author wasn't wise enough to see. It should also increase sales substantially.

I am indebted for some of the material to two people I've never met. Chief among them is Max Eastman, whose 1936 book, *Enjoyment of Laughter,* both entertains and provokes. Eastman gives us permission to laugh for the heck of it, with or without Deeper Meanings.

Conrad Hyers, on the other hand, is keenly aware of the theological implications of humor. The anthology he edited, *Holy Laughter,* and his more recent book, *The Comic Vision and the Christian Faith,* enabled me to see ways in which humor is linked to faith. Quotations from people like Hyers and Peter Berger also added literary dignity which the book sorely needed.

Thanks are due Mary Ann Martin, whom I met while I was giving the 1980 Carrington Lecture at Southwest Missouri State University. She challenged me to write a "theological treatise" on humor, and this is it—warts and all. Her letter provided several excellent quotations for chapters four and five and convinced me that Roman Catholics have more fun than Quakers. Perhaps that is why there are so many more of them.

Debby Toschlog typed the manuscript and corrected my errors, an achievement which saved me considerable embarrassment and added to the life span of Word editors.

Finally, my wife Nancy and our children Sarah, Martha, Brett, and Ruth deserve thanks. Their words and deeds continue to provide plenty of reasons for laughter and tears. The book is dedicated to Nancy, partly because it was completed on our twenty-fifth wedding anniversary. Mainly, however, it is dedicated to her because of what those twenty-five years represent. To have married a woman who is pretty, intelligent, and able to laugh at bad jokes is to be richly blessed. Nancy continues to think I am wonderful, a source of poorly disguised amusement to others and unending encouragement to me.

TOM MULLEN

PART ONE

WHY LAUGH?

1

Funny Things Happen

An engineer, a psychologist, and a theologian were hunting in the wilds of northern Canada. They came across an isolated cabin, far removed from any town. Because friendly hospitality is a virtue practiced by those who live in the wilderness, the hunters knocked on the door to ask permission to rest.

No one answered their knocks, but, discovering the cabin was unlocked, they entered. It was a simple place—two rooms with a minimum of furniture and household equipment. Nothing was surprising about the cabin except the stove. It was large, potbellied, and made of cast iron. What was unusual was its location: it was suspended in midair by wires attached to the ceiling beams.

"Fascinating," said the psychologist. "It is obvious that this lonely trapper, isolated from humanity, has elevated his stove so he can curl up under it and vicariously experience a return to the womb."

"Nonsense!" replied the engineer. "The man is practic-ing laws of thermodynamics. By elevating his stove, he has discovered a way to distribute heat more evenly throughout the cabin."

*"With all due respect," interrupted the theologian, "I'm sure that hanging his stove from the ceiling has religious meaning. Fire **lifted up** has been a religious symbol for centuries."*

The three debated the point for several minutes without resolving the issue. When the trapper finally returned, they immediately asked him why he had hung his heavy potbel-lied stove by wires from the ceiling.

His answer was succinct: "Had plenty of wire, not much stove pipe."

Examining life for Deeper Meanings is a twen-tieth-century preoccupation. We assume that things are not what they seem. Words disguise Hidden Feelings. Actions symbolize Something Else. Even jokes are viewed as devices for signaling aggression or passivity, superiority or inferiority, sexual release or sexual repression.

Such analysis is partly correct. This book is about humor and its end result, laughter—and both can be surface expressions of hidden feelings or thoughts. We tell a joke to cover up our nervousness, or we laugh at a story we don't understand to disguise feel-ing stupid.

Many assume humor is *only* a manipulative tech-nique. Speakers *warm up* their audiences with jokes before they get down to business. One professional humorist in California supplements his income by going over the lectures of college professors, insert-ing funny lines to enliven them. (We know several teachers who could use his services.) Humorous speakers are frequently contacted with a similar request: "Would you give me a couple of jokes to jazz up my speech on taxidermy? I don't want to sound stuffy."

Others cite the power of humor to reduce tension. They remind us how movie audiences burst into nervous laughter right after the heroine escapes decapitation. For example, in the movie *The Shining*, touted as the scariest film ever made, the psychotic father attempts to break into a room in order to kill his wife. As he viciously attacks the door with an ax, he calls out, "Honey, I'm home!" The audience roars in relieved laughter.

Indeed, sociologists have studied with great seriousness the purposes of humor in a variety of cultures. Their research includes such rib-tickling conclusions as the following:

Hammond related these situational features in his conception of joking among the West African Mossi as an adaptive mechanism which assumes importance for the way in which it provides for the catharsis of potentially disruptive emotions.[1]

Hammond discovered, in other words, that the West African Mossi laughed about their differences instead of bashing someone with a club.

Sigmund Freud, well known for his ability to find Deeper Meanings in dreams, habits, and nearly everything else, found a whole bunch of significance in jokes.[2] He thought humor was inevitably used for a psychological purpose—to degrade or intimidate, to disguise or compensate, to express or deny a subconscious feeling. Jokes were used for all kinds of high and low reasons save one—having fun for its own sake. For Freud, there was no such thing as pure nonsense.

I disagree. While it is obvious that humor and its result, laughter, are powerful means to many conscious and subconscious ends; to deny the validity of laughter for its own sake is to be the victim of a bad joke. When we experience humor *only* as manipulation or compensation, we damage our ability to laugh at funny things, of which there are a great many in life. Down deep, there is a need for shallowness.

Life is full of incongruities, many of which defy analysis but invite laughter. Jokes that produce laughter usually reflect those incongruities. For example:

Question: Do you know the difference between a fly and a bee?
Answer: You don't have to zip up a bee!

A dumb joke. Yet grown people have laughed at that joke—aloud and in the presence of witnesses. Its dumbness defies analysis, and our attempts to analyze transform us into comic characters. ("Obviously, the reference to the fly in the above context indicates a concealed sexual reference, a topic we were not allowed to discuss as children." "On the contrary, the pun suggests how humans abhor insects. Thus, by making them objects of a joke, we dissipate our repulsion.")

Wrong. What is there is all there is. It's funny because it's funny. There is plenty of wire, not enough stovepipe. Laughter for its own sake, words and deeds that strike us as funny, jokes that tickle our ribs but defy explanation—all argue that humor is its own excuse for being.

To claim too much for humor, of course, is as incorrect as to reduce its value to mere utility. Claiming too much, however, is not our problem. I cleverly put this chapter first because its point is basic: humorous laughter is a gift God has given humanity.

Contrary to popular opinion, the funniest jokes are not made up; they are discovered. A sense of humor is the gift of observing the passing parade and laughing at appropriate moments. Life itself provides the raw material for laughter, and the rewards of a sense of humor are many. Those with eyes to see and ears to hear will discover opportunities for grins and guffaws, snickers and titters, chuckles and side-splitting, tear-bringing, body-shaking howls.

God has given us permission to enjoy incongruities, absurdities, and other normal experiences. Thus, sex is funny, religion can be either high or low comedy, and race is sometimes hilarious. They're also serious. The issue is when and how to laugh, and we are given no neat formula that enables us to decide.

For now, we can settle for accepting humor as a gift from God. Sometimes we laugh for sinister motives, and sometimes we use humor for noble reasons. But, thank God, often we laugh for the same reason fishermen fish—for the halibut. Life is serious, and in the back of our minds we recall we're eventually heading for the cemetery. Fortunately, the Christian faith says the graveyard is not the last stop. Thus, we are free to enjoy funny things that happen along the way.

Resources for Discussion

1. The author says the joke about a fly and a bee is dumb but funny. If you found it amusing, why? Does there have to be an explanation for the jokes and stories at which we laugh?
2. Do you agree that there is such a thing as "pure nonsense"? Can you recall an anecdote that was totally illogical or silly, yet made you laugh?
3. Elephant jokes are usually told by children but are secretly laughed at by grownups. Consider the following:

   (a) How can you tell if there's an elephant in the refrigerator?
   By the footprints in the peanut butter.

   (b) How do you get down off an elephant?
   You don't get down off an elephant; you get down off a duck.

   (c) How do you stop a herd of elephants from charging?
   You take away their credit cards.

   (d) What do you get if you cross a chicken with an elephant?
   Whatever it is, Colonel Sanders will have trouble dipping it in the batter.

   Did you laugh at these jokes? Or groan, which is an outer and visible sign of an inner and mystical chuckle? Why? (Who cares why?)
4. The author says humor is a gift from God. Is the ability to laugh a talent (gift) in the way a pleasant singing voice and quick reflexes are gifts? Do

some have it and some not? Or is a sense of humor a gift that all people have but some fail to develop?

5. Do you have a sense of humor? Do you laugh easily or sparingly? Why are some persons "extra" serious about life?

2

On Children and Cows

Being "in fun" is a condition most natural to childhood. . . . Children at play reveal the humorous laugh at its simplest and most omnivorous form. To them every untoward, unprepared for, unmanageable, inauspicious, ugly, disgusting, puzzling, startling, deceiving, shaking, blinding, jolting, deafening, banging, bumping, or otherwise shocking and disturbing thing, unless it be calamitous enough to force them out of the mood of play, is enjoyable as funny.[1]

Babies are not much interested in Deeper Meanings. So long as their tummies are filled and their diapers are not, they personify playfulness. In learning to walk a child will delight at mishaps, such as sitting down with a thud, and gurgle in uproarious merriment. As Max Eastman says, almost any would-be disaster—unless it really hurts—has potential for laughter.

Commercial enterprises that prey on new parents hide this truth. They want to sell us fifty-dollar panda bears that stare or supersonic robots that go glug-a-boom. They provide us with an unending parade of novelties, all of which can be explained by mechanics and all of which eventually become stale.

Babies don't need all that stuff. Parents, uncles, and aunts buy it because they want to do a nice thing, but small children are content with delights provided free of charge by the universe. They grin and slobber instinctively in the midst of tiny tragedies. Where is the infant so serious that he can't muster a grin after falling down when trying to stand? Why does a little girl squeal with delight when her father plays peekaboo for the umpteenth time? But then, why shouldn't she? After all, a grown man in his best suit popping out from behind the sofa and making grotesque faces for the sole purpose of seeing an infant giggle—now, that's funny!

Parents usually recognize a happy child when they see, hear, and clean up after one. Spilled milk is regarded by few children as a calamity. In fact, most babies enjoy the act and aftermath of spilling it, at least until their parents conclude such behavior indicates character disorder—and respond accordingly. Children teach us that pleasant things are to be enjoyed and disagreeable things, so long as they don't "spoil the fun," acquire a pleasant flavor and provoke a laugh.

Which brings us to cows. Cows are funny in their own right. They do not try to be amusing, and their behavior provides few profound philosophical insights. Children, in a state of fun, see that cows (and pigs, puppies, and worms) are funny. Our son Brett, when he was four, once doubled over in laughter while watching the rear-view of a cow walking. The combination of its side-to-side gait, its clanking bell, and its occasional pauses to turn and glance at us, while patiently chewing its cud, was funny. It was not trying to be humorous, nor was it attempting to manipulate us in any way. It was just plain funny, and a four-year-old noticed and laughed.

I thought I had discovered an important insight— cows are amusing! While not as significant as the law of gravity or the invention of the wheel, realizing cows were inherently funny creatures was not too shabby a discovery for a lazy summer afternoon.

Alas! Others before me had already seen what Brett had seen—some setting their discoveries to verse. Arthur Guiterman's "Ode to a Cow" is a case in point:

> The cautious, collapsible cow
> gives milk by the sweat of her brow;
> then under the trees,
> she folds her front knees
> and sits fore and aft with a bow.[2]

In similar fashion Gelett Burgess knew cows were funny when he saw one—or rather didn't see one— or . . . heck, read his poem:

> I never saw a purple cow,
> I never hope to see one;
> But this I'll tell you, anyhow
> I'd rather see than be one.[3]

WHY LAUGH?

Ogden Nash, that great describer of things funny which do not necessarily have Deeper Meanings, also knew cows were entertaining. His eulogy of them is succinct:

> The cow is of the bovine ilk;
> One end is moo, the other, milk.[4]

Children and occasional adults like Guiterman, Burgess, and Nash do not create humor. They identify matters worth laughing about which were funny all along, but which most of us failed to notice. Those able to laugh spontaneously at cows, pigs, puppies, and worms can sometimes move on to Advanced Laughing 201. Adult laughing depends upon a childlike perspective, but our training and conditioning into maturity works against it. We learn to analyze before we laugh and, as a consequence, laugh less and maybe not at all. We experience the paralysis of analysis. Many tiptoe through life with as much mirth as a sexton tolling his own funeral bell.

If humor and laughter are gifts from God, however, losing the ability to laugh is poor stewardship. Our efforts to be adults are strenuous and involve patching, prodding, and fixing. Sometimes we can't hold it in any longer, and laughter bursts forth without cause nor for any Freudian reason. We may be embarrassed by our spontaneous laughter, and afterwards we may wish we had kept a straight face. Nevertheless, occasionally our "inner child" takes over and decorum loses the day.

A case in point: a friend and I were sitting in a Thanksgiving worship service. The sermon was about commitment and how we put too many conditions on what we do for others. To illustrate his point, the preacher told an old story about a man who helped his brother-in-law start a business, buy a house, and educate his children. When the brother-in-law requested further help to expand his business, the man refused, feeling he had done enough. His refusal was met with great indignation, so he reminded his brother-in-law of the several generous gifts he had made over the years. To this the angry brother-in-law replied, "Yes, but what have you done for me recently?"

It was a mild and harmless joke, the kind that gets a small laugh from congregations wired for small laughter. The preacher went on, however, to elaborate. "We are often like that brother-in-law," he said, "always saying 'yes, but.' Again and again we, too, fall back on our buts."

A small *faux pas,* a slip of the tongue, a tiny blemish on the face of a sermon. Whatever it was, for the two of us it represented the end of attentive listening. Throughout the rest of the sermon, the offering, all four verses of the closing hymn, and the benediction, we struggled for composure. Tears poured from our eyes. Our bodies trembled. One of us would attempt to disguise our convulsions by pretending to blow his nose—which merely incited the other to greater internal spasms of laughter. Our stomachs knotted in agony and our bladders cried for relief.

When the service was finally, mercifully over, we dashed out a side door to a small courtyard where we could let the dam burst. For half an hour we laughed. We snorted, hee-hawed, and bellowed. We paused for breath, only to break into more gales of mirth. We literally exhausted ourselves laughing.

That event occurred over twenty-five years ago. Yet whenever my friend and I renew our acquaintance, we both recall that night. The irony is that no one else, so far as we could tell, thought the preacher's remark was funny at all. A greater irony is that it wasn't *that* funny!

Laughter dwells within most of us, and adults discipline themselves to suppress it. The result is that we deny ourselves the fun of being "in fun." But, while I do not recommend uncontrolled laughter as a proper response in worship, I argue that being "in fun" is a gift from God. It is a prerequisite for laughter. It is looking at the world with a vision slightly askew. It is the exercise of playfulness. When we are in this state, good humor radiates through us, makes us happy, and gives us joyful illumination of the disharmonies of human life.

When we are in a state of fun, we are probably not in a mood to save the world—nor destroy it. But we may be able to do one Good Thing—enjoy a moment of the time God has given us.

Resources for Discussion

1. What does the author mean by being "in fun"?
   Under what circumstances are you most able to
   be "in fun"? On vacation? When you are with certain people? When life at home and at work are
   free of worries? Most of the time?
2. The author says that things worth laughing about
   are present all the time, but most adults fail to
   notice them. What are events or situations you
   discovered that tickled your funny bone but came
   without warning into your experience? Did the
   other people around you also find them amusing,
   or did some regard them as deadly serious?
3. Does the process of growing into adulthood condition us *out* of a humorous perspective? Why do
   children laugh at things adults fail to find the
   least bit funny—such as spilled milk?
4. Think of a time when you wanted desperately to
   laugh but it seemed inappropriate to do so—for
   instance, when you were sitting in church. What
   did it feel like? What were your reasons for sup-
   pressing laughter? By continually resisting the
   urge to laugh aloud, do we stifle our ability to be
   "in fun"?
5. The author says it is "poor stewardship" to let too
   many of life's foibles pass by without laughing.
   What does he mean? Do you agree?
6. Why are the *Peanuts* and *Garfield* comic strips
   popular with millions? Are children in comic
   strips able to "get away" with funny insights that

real-world adults are hesitant to share? What dimensions of human nature does Garfield the cat represent? Why is he funny?

3

Please, God, May
We Laugh?

Christians are not well known for their ability to laugh. Our reputation centers about a *serious* call to a devout and holy life, and certain kinds of Christians (for example, Puritans) are stereotypes of a dark and somber faith. H. L. Mencken said that "puritans carry the haunting fear that someone, somewhere is having a good time." By "puritan" he obviously meant religious people in general, not just those old folks in strange hats, white collars, and gray knickers.

Do we deserve such a sour reputation? Our immediate response is to say "no." After all, we sing of having "joy, joy, joy, joy down in our hearts." In a society which promotes the pursuit of happiness as a constitutional right, to be against fun is as bad as opposing baseball, hot dogs, apple pie, and Chevrolet.

Most sermons include three points, three jokes, and a poem. Some congregations, furthermore, are so loosey-goosey they "celebrate" in worship and blow up balloons with smiley faces drawn on them. Christians opposed to laughter!?! Get serious, friend!

Indeed, getting serious about humor has been a trademark of the faithful for generations. Early Christians were highly suspicious of laughter, and contemporary religious writers appreciate humor primarily for weighty reasons. "Joy" is allowed, nay, encouraged, but it clearly means something serious. Reinhold Niebuhr illustrates this mood: "The genuine joy of reconciliation with God, which is possible only as the fruit of genuine repentance, is *a joy which stands beyond laughter*[1] (italics mine).

Niebuhr's point of view, as serious as it is, represents more tolerance of humor than many early church leaders had. Way back in the fourth century Bishop Ambrose pooped a lot of parties with admonitions like this: "Joking should be avoided even in small talk, so that some more serious topic is not made light of. 'Woe upon you who laugh now; you shall mourn and weep,' (Luke 6:25) saith the Lord. Are we looking for something to laugh at, so that we may laugh now but weep hereafter? I maintain that not only loose jokes but jokes of any kind must be avoided—except perhaps when our words are full of sweetness and grace, not indelicate."[2]

Bishop Ambrose was no fun at all, much to his delight.

Others among that great cloud of witnesses join him as guardians against mirth. Robert Barclay, a seventeenth-century Quaker theologian, showed that the grimness of the fathers is visited upon their children. Barclay wrote, "It is not lawful to use games, sports, plays, nor among other things comedies among Christians, under the notion of recreations which do not agree with Christian silence, gravity, and sobriety; for laughing, sporting, gaming, mocking, jesting, vain talking, etc. is not Christian liberty, nor harmless mirth."[3]

Barclay would have had a fit upon seeing the smiling Quaker on the oats box. Even so, he was ahead of his times in identifying games and sports as inappropriate recreation. All Little League coaches or Indiana basketball fans know their games have nothing to do with fun but are Deadly Serious. Still, to include "laughing" and "jesting" in his blanket condemnation adds to Christianity's reputation for sourness.

Real Christians don't fool around. They write essays on the Comic Vision or deal with the ontology of humor, whatever that is. They're concerned with Comic Eschatology, a theme which by its very wording warns against laughter. Chad Walsh hit the thumb on the nail when he wrote an essay about faith and humor. He said: "The problem with most essays on the comic . . . is that they proceed in a solemnity of tone and style more suited to earning a degree in philosophy or being named bishop than inviting us to celebration and laughter."[4]

He's right. Christians carry a vague but persistent uneasiness about humor. Merriment is more at home in the pool hall than the church. Christians are wary of too much laughter, limiting themselves most of the time to two jokes, one spouse, and no drinks. Humor is—how shall we put it—less responsible than seriousness.

WHY LAUGH?

Let the record show that Christians have good reason to be serious. As an old joke says, "If you can keep your head while all others are losing theirs, it may be that you have not fully assessed the situation." Laughing because we are unwilling to deal with serious matters is a serious matter. It is a distortion of reality.

But so is the exclusion of humorous laughter. Humor has the power to hurt and heal. It provides a perspective that has serious implications. A comic vision is kin to a tragic vision.

Christianity's longstanding uneasiness with humorous laughter, however, has caused us to neglect nurturing a capacity for being "in fun." That capacity, as we have seen, is a condition most natural to childhood, and adults retain the aptitude for being "in fun" in lesser degrees. Some stifle it completely. Raymond Moody, a medical doctor, identifies certain persons as "laughter resistant." Such individuals are forever misunderstanding humor by taking remarks spoken in jest as though they were intended to be serious.[5] "Laughter resistance" (or impaired comic vision) may be a vocational hazard for Christians.

I contend, however, that being "in fun" is not a pause for breath before we get back to living life as Christians. It is part of the pilgrimage. Enjoying the enjoyable is a matter of right use of our resources. As Conrad Hyers says, "Humor apart from holiness may be irresponsible; but holiness apart from humor is inhuman."[6]

Children learn about tragedy and pain in the process of growing up, and they are usually able to recognize the humor that goes hand in hand with that pain. We don't have to teach them *when* to laugh but when *not* to laugh. A dignified man slips on the ice and that's funny. He may have bruised his tailbone, but it's still funny to us. We do stupid things that have serious consequences and somebody, somewhere, laughs at our fumbles.

And why not? Down through the ages, what have most jokes been about? Unpaid bills, bad taste, pomposity, drunks, taxes, going to the bathroom, sexual inadequacy, stinginess, and stupidity. Not to mention mothers-in-law, corpses, politicians, and tramps. These matters have to do with unpleasantness, yet they are the stuff of which jokes are made.

A Christian perspective sees *both* the sorrow *and* the humor of life, sometimes in the same event. Consider the following, all of which were reported in the press:

—A powerful congressman gets involved with a striptease dancer named Fanne Fox. His affair is discovered after he gets drunk and is arrested while frolicking in a public fountain in Washington. Laughing is as appropriate a response to such goings-on as is righteous indignation.

—A music company produces records consisting of four minutes of silence for playing on restaurant juke boxes. This is a commentary on our life and times and worth a chuckle to those whose comic vision is unimpaired.

—In Calgary, Alberta, a forty-year-old construction worker became the first Black man ever to join the Ku Klux Klan. (Do you suppose they recruited him to wash the sheets?)

—A Baptist minister in Grand Rapids used a twelve-volt battery to shock his students as he delivered his message to them in Bible school. He said: "God tells us to do something or suffer the consequences." Is this tragedy or comedy?

—An undertaker in Georgia opens a drive-in funeral home so that mourners can gear down and pay their respects. Do we laugh or weep?

—New York prostitutes unionize for better working conditions and better treatment from the police. What can we say?

—A national magazine reveals model Cheryl Tiegs is a Quaker. (This should not surprise us. She frequently appears on magazine covers *very* simply dressed.) How about that, Robert Barclay?

All of the above are both sad and funny. Wilbur Mills's career was ruined by the Fanne Fox affair, and compassion reminds us that personal tragedy is no laughing matter. But, doggone it, the event is still funny! There are probably good reasons for record companies producing the soundlessness of silence and for funeral homes to encourage drive-in calling. Still, can we keep from laughing as we imagine somber morticians, dressed in black, recording our condolences as we express them from a red Volkswagen?

Professional humorists observe that much of American life is self-parody, particularly that which borders on the tragic. They don't have to think up jokes. They merely expose jokes that are there. In similar fashion a Christian perspective expands on the experience of being "in fun." It allows us to laugh until we cry or cry until we laugh.

Such a perspective is worth having, particularly when we slip on the ice. We not only provide a laugh to someone else, we do a favor for ourselves. After we have rubbed the sore places, checked for bruises, and counted all our parts, we make a significant discovery: we're still alive! That's worth a laugh—and a huge sigh of relief!

Resources for Discussion

1. Do you agree that Christians have a reputation for being somber, even opposed to having fun? To the extent that such a reputation is true, on what is it based?
2. Consider the following comments:

   (a) A boy, upon returning home from his first circus, said, "Once you've been to a circus, you'll never enjoy prayer meeting again!"
   (b) A mountaineer, after returning from Europe following World War I, remarked, "I shore wisht I'd seen Paris before I was converted."

   Does the Christian faith put limits on fun? Does your denomination stress self-denial? Does self-denial work against having fun? Is there a Christian definition of "fun" that is different from a secular understanding?
3. Is humor "less responsible" than seriousness?
4. The author says we don't have to teach children when to laugh but when *not* to laugh. Do you agree? Why or why not?
5. What does Conrad Hyers mean when he says "humor apart from holiness may be irresponsible; but holiness apart from humor is inhuman"?
6. Consider the list of comic-tragic events the author lists. What is your reaction to them? Amusement? Disgust? Anger? Which, for you, are mostly tragic? Which are mostly comic? Are there similar events you would add to the list?

7. What is your reaction to the following: A minister in Niles, Ohio denounced the Easter bunny as a pagan god and burned a giant fake rabbit in the town square.

4

Smile When You
Say That!

Humor is playfulness. Humor is being "in fun." All attempts to explain it inevitably fail in the same way defining horseplay fails. Those in the mood of play will laugh for any reason, good or bad. Those in a serious mood will watch a baby smile and assume it is feeling gas pains. They will be treated to a rear-end view of a cow walking and draw no human comparisons, even though it looks a lot like the rear view of Uncle Charlie.

The key is a playful mood. Human beings are united, drawn closer, by personal tragedy. The community gathers around mourners and shares their grief. The tragic mood is vicariously shared, and in some mystical way this helps dissipate sorrow. In similar fashion those who laugh together are, for the moment at least, brothers and sisters.

WHY LAUGH?

Good humor depends upon good relationships. In Owen Wistar's novel, *The Virginian*, the hero is confronted by a man who calls him a dirty name. Six-shooter at the ready, the Virginian replies: "When you call me that, smile!" Subtract the six-shooter, and that scene is repeated at reunions, homecomings, and parties all over the land.

We greet old friends with playful insults:

"George, you old horsethief! I believe you've gotten uglier!"

"Mary, I love your hair. Where did you get it?"

We do not usually greet strangers with accusations of theft or call attention to their ugliness or loss of hair. Nor will smiles, no matter how broad, compensate for a positive relationship if it is absent. In fact, without (1) a positive, friendly relationship and (2) a Mark Twain called "a misunderstanding conducted with crowbars."

An early study of infant behavior made the same point.[1] Mothers of infants could tease and tickle them into laughter fifteen times as often as a stranger could. A mother's tickle produced a smile, giggle, or laugh. A stranger's tickle usually got a negative reaction—whining, fussing, or crying. The babies, as it were, could "take a joke" from their mothers but not from strangers. Had they been able to articulate their feelings, they would have said, "Because it's mom and she's smiling, I'll laugh along."

"Laughing with" presupposes "laughing" (a playful mood) and "with-ness" (a positive relationship). Dorothy Parker, the famous humorist, said, "The funny people you like best are the ones you laugh with. There's [Robert] Benchley, for instance. You live through his troubles with him—they are your own troubles—and that is why you enjoy them so particularly." Most of us have favorite comedians (Bill Cosby is mine), and they become like old friends. Though we've never met them, we identify with them in laughter.

"Laughing at" is humor at the expense of someone else, but "laughing with" builds sympathy with another. We become kindred spirits. "Laughing with" does not alienate us from others; it does not identify enemies. It identifies our friends and how funny they are.

Clifton Fadiman said it well: "[Great humor] proceeds out of a kind of wistful affection for the human race, an affection that wishes the race were better than it is. Such humor measures the distance between what we are and what we could be. It is a kind of message sent out from one person to another and it says: 'You are awfully funny, but so am I, so let's get together.' That kind of humor unites rather than divides."[2]

Enjoying each other's company involves more than humor, of course, but an *inability* to laugh together precludes a complete relationship. Husbands and wives cultivate their relationship with private jokes and the discovery that they both laugh at the same things. Courtship often focuses on laughing together as a primary form of attraction. How can we not be attracted to someone who has the good judgment, taste, and sensitivity to laugh at our jokes?

Indeed, one of the most positive features of the woman I married was her ready laughter, particularly at my unquestionably entertaining stories. A pretty woman, she had a gift for laughter that enhanced her beauty, and her appreciation of my humorous stuff was a convincing reason for marriage. We were married for five years before I realized she laughed at everybody's humorous stuff.

"Laughing with" both cultivates and depends upon intimacy. Shared humor becomes shared experience, and relationships are nurtured by celebrating words and deeds that induce another to laugh. As Evelyn Waugh said, "We cherish our friends not for their ability to amuse us, but for our ability to amuse them."

"Laughing with" builds bridges across racial and ethnic barriers, too. If we are white, we know we have a good relationship with a black friend when we are able to share gentle racial jokes. I feel complimented (I think) by a black friend who sometimes refers to me as his favorite honkey. He says he likes my looks, but they would be better if I had a little color in my cheeks—and the rest of my body as well. In turn, I invite him to shuffle over to our house for dinner in his rented Cadillac.

Our conversations are not always at such a high level, but the racial jokes between us illustrate a point. Neither of us would make such comments to other black or white persons we did not know so well. Furthermore, we both are poking fun at something else that is absurd—namely, racial stereotypes. Intimacy, trust, and mutual respect provide the context for entering into fun about race.

"Laughing with" can also bridge religious differences, but the same risks—hurting or offending—prevail, and the same rules—trust and a playful mood—apply. While speaking at an ecumenical gathering on the healing and hurting powers of humor, I mentioned a newspaper article describing a Roman Catholic parish in which a drive-in confessional was used. I suggested the practice might be called "toot and tell."

The comment got the intended result, hearty laughter, but in the informal discussion after the speech, I met a delightful woman who identified herself as Roman Catholic. I asked her if she had been offended by my story, and she assured me she had not. Several days later, however, I received a letter from her with the following comments:

> I am the lady who asked you to autograph a book for the priest at the lecture last night. I am also the one who said she was not offended by your story about drive-in confessions. Now I must admit I lied. I *was* offended—or at least I felt very uncomfortable.

> Here's why: I didn't know you or anything about your attitude toward my beloved Holy Mother Church, so I had no way of surmising whether you were laughing *with* us or *at* us. Were you a Catholic, everybody (with some lamentable exceptions) would have split his sides laughing.

> One of the most precious things to me about the Roman Church is her well-documented and historical capacity for laughing at herself and her children. But, laughter from a stranger is not the same comfortably affectionate matter as laughing at one's own foibles and those of one's cherished family members and dear friends.

The woman's insight was absolutely correct. Humor can make things worse and it can offend— UNLESS we already trust one another and share a playful spirit. This woman demonstrated sufficient trust to write her letter, and she clearly possessed a playful spirit. Enclosed in the envelope was a religious medal accompanied by these words: "This is a 35-cent St. Dymphna medal (unblessed). She is the patron saint of lunatics. *Everybody* should have a St. Dymphna medal these days."

If St. Dymphna medals were able to release special powers, one improvement in the world would surely be forthcoming. We might trust each other enough to laugh with all kinds of people—different races, other religious groups, maybe even our enemies. Certainly being *unable* to laugh with others different from us makes things worse. There is no humor in slogans like "Love it or Leave it" or "All Power to the People." There is only what Milton Mayer calls "unrelived earnestness," for which laughter is the only cure.

"Laughing with" unites, binds, and overcomes. It doesn't necessarily solve problems nor resolve conflicts, but it helps build trust out of which kinship can develop. During the late sixties, a time when "unrelieved earnestness" had become a way of life on college campuses, the generations glared at each other daily across well-defined battle lines. At one university where administrators and students had confronted each other for over a week, the middle-aged chaplain was asked to begin a negotiating session with prayer. The words of his prayer didn't resolve the differences between the two groups, but they were a start.

The chaplain prayed: "O God, bless those here with long hair and all those with short hair, and all those with no hair, and help them to love each other, for Christ's sake. Amen."

Amen, indeed.

Resources for Discussion

1. Why do good friends enjoy playful insults and teasing? Is it a way of being intimate without getting mushy? Is it a means of "testing" a friendship?
2. Who is your favorite comedian? Do you identify with him or her? For example, Erma Bombeck has a huge following because thousands laugh with *her* at *their* similar circumstances. Others laughed at Jack Benny because he was the butt of his own jokes most of the time. We, in other words, laughed *at* him *with* him.
3. Consider the comments the author makes about racial humor. Do you have friends of other races with whom you can share racial or ethnic jokes? Did you ever tell such a joke and discover your relationship was not strong enough to allow it to be told without offense? Should racial jokes ever be told outside the intimacy of a close, trusting relationship?
4. What is meant by "unrelieved earnestness"? How is it an enemy of intimacy? Why does the author say laughter is its only cure?
5. Does laughing together *build* trust or *depend* upon trust already built?
6. Consider the story about "toot and tell." Should that joke have been told at an ecumenical gathering? What are examples of stories that are *inclusive* (rather than confrontive) about race and/or religion? How do we decide which ones are acceptable?

7. Examine the cartoon printed below. Do you find it funny? What is its point? Does it "put down" the Methodists? Does it tease Methodists about one of their strengths, i.e. their ability to include diverse theological views?

"O, Great Motage, Protector of humble men, Descendant of the Great Fish, Father of the Most Terrible Volcano and Devourer of All Enemies, we humbly beg your leave to join with the Methodists."

Clayton D. Powers

5

Oh, What a Relief
It Is!

In Mark Twain's novel, *Tom Sawyer Abroad*, the main characters are riding in a balloon. It lands in a forsaken desert, and several lions come after them. They barely manage to get back into the balloon and escape. As they float away, Tom Sawyer looks down at the disappointed lions and says, "I couldn't help seeing their side of it."

Those able to see the humor of a situation are usually more understanding of the human condition than those who can't. Seeing the funny or ironic side of events is a way of seeing the truth they contain. An inability to laugh at human foibles is blasphemy. It treats human beings as if they were godlike, and they aren't. I foul up. You foul up. All God's children foul up, and laughing about our foibles is a form of confession.

Consider the Pharisee in Luke 18:11–12. Clearly, he is a pompous fool: "God, I thank thee, that I am not as other men are, extortioners, unjust, adulterers, or even as this publican. I fast twice in the week, I give tithes of that I possess." His lack of humility is obvious, and it is hard to imagine his having a sense of humor. It is inconceivable that the Pharisee in this story would laugh at himself. When humility is missing, perspective about ourselves is missing. An absence of humor leads to the same result.

The Roman Catholic woman quoted earlier recognized this. She wrote, "Do you know what I often pray, Dr. Mullen? I pray to the Holy Spirit for funny things to happen to me and to others in distress. . . . I am convinced that real humility simply consists of the capacity to recognize and laugh at one's own pride and vanity. Humor is nothing short of grace to see ourselves as we really are. Oh, what a relief it is!"

Relief results both from formal confession—"God, be merciful to me, a sinner"—and informal confession—poking fun at our pretensions. Those able to laugh at themselves find relief, and they release others around them to do the same.

My religious denomination is the Society of Friends (Quaker). I wasn't always a Friend; I joined because I heard that was where the big money was. That proved to be wrong, but I learned upon joining Quakers that they attack large social and moral problems with conscientious determination. They work for peace—and if you really want to cause conflict, work for peace. They seek to thwart aggression wherever they find it, and they aggressively seek it out. In short, because Quakers are so serious about their religious concerns, they need a humorous perspective about themselves.

Fortunately, some Friends have been able to keep perspective by laughing at themselves—even at their weightiest concerns. A long-standing Quaker joke illustrates the point. A Friend is awakened in the middle of the night to discover a burglar in the house. Quietly he gets his hunting rifle off the wall and confronts the thief. "Friend, robber," he says, "I would not harm thee for the world, but thou standest where I am about to shoot!"

That joke is best told by Quakers about Quakers because it suggests an important truth: nonviolence is an important virtue in a violent world, but it is difficult to practice consistently. Religious people seldom laugh easily at their most deeply held convictions, because they do not want to demean these beliefs or deny their importance. The point, however, is this: an inability to laugh about our concerns too often results in idolatry of the cause.

True Believers need the perspective humor provides. Otherwise, they become as self-righteous and unfunny as Luke's Pharisee. Reinhold Niebuhr, who is seldom accused of being frivolous, agrees:

> Humor is a proof of the capacity of the self to gain a vantage point from which it is able to look at itself. The sense of humor is thus a by-product of self-transcendence. . . .All of us ought to be ready to laugh at ourselves because all of us are a little funny in our foibles, conceits, and pretensions. What is funny about us is precisely that we take ourselves too seriously. We are rather insignificant little bundles of energy and vitality in a vast organization of life. But we pretend that we are the very center of this organi-

zation. This pretension is ludicrous; and its absurdity increases with our lack of awareness of it. The less we are able to laugh at ourselves the more it becomes necessary and inevitable that others laugh at us.[1]

The more intense our involvement in a cause, the greater the need for a humorous perspective. If Karl Marx's revolution had had a healthy dose of Groucho Marx's comedy, lives would have been saved—and the resulting regime would probably have been more humane.

Jokes about the temperance movement abound, many of which deliberately ridicule teetotalers. Teetotalers who can poke fun at themselves, however, disarm that legion of persons wary of the tendency for abstinence to turn into self-righteousness. Quakers are not so well known for temperance as, say, Methodists or Baptists, but they make better characters in jokes because they talk funny. The story goes that one Friend was particularly adamant against the use of booze and seldom let an opportunity pass for speaking against demon rum. His conversation was loaded with rantings about liquor, and he became such a boor that acquaintances were nearly driven to drink.

One night four of them came across him while he was walking home. Their courage had been fortified by libations provided in a local tavern, so they decided to teach the old Quaker a lesson. They grabbed him, held a bottle in front of his face, and insisted he take a drink.

"Never," he replied, clamping his lips shut like a vise. Whereupon the four men wrestled him to the ground and again insisted he take a swig, which he steadfastly refused. This time one of the men produced a funnel, forced it into the old Quaker's mouth, and poured a generous portion down his throat.

"Now, old Quaker, will you take a drink?"

He, sputtering and choking, replied: "Never will I take a drink. But thee may funnel me again."

That joke may be suspect because it implies that people would be happier if they drank liquor. However, it also identifies the self-righteous spirit that has plagued the temperance movement, and it offers a corrective.

The feminist movement is a serious cause for many Christians. Its True Believers brought passion and dedication to the effort to pass the Equal Rights Amendment. Their opponents charged the ERA would force men and women to use the same public restrooms. Feminists usually responded with rage. The charge, however, was absurd and deserved a humorous response. ("My husband won't stand for it. He has three daughters and a wife, and it takes so long now for him to get into the bathroom, he often leaves home to find an available toilet.")

The Moral Majority as a movement is funnier than it knows. The intensity of its True Believers makes Carrie Nation look like a bartender. Ecologists and nuclear disarmament advocates, in my opinion, are right in their concerns, but their urgency is often higher-pitched than a squeaky violin.

Careful readers will note that both conservative and liberal causes were used above as illustrations. That was deliberate because the need is to laugh at ourselves in the middle of our own crusades, not somebody else's. As in the case of Tom Sawyer escaping from lions, humor helps us see another side of an issue.

WHY LAUGH?

The one offense which a sense of humor cannot tolerate is that we forget our humanity—the finite quality of our most deeply cherished causes. Laughing at ourselves frees religious people to be cheerful crusaders. It enables us to laugh in the heat of our commitment to noble causes and in the battle against evil. Laughing at ourselves is possible when we are able to see humanity as it is—a little lower than the angels and at times only slightly higher than the apes.

Mark Twain is remembered as a humorist, but he was also a cheerful crusader because he had an affectionate concern for people, flawed though they be. He once commented, "I'm quite sure that I have no race prejudices, and I think I have no color prejudices nor caste nor creed prejudices. . . . I can stand any society. All that I care to know is that people are human beings. That's enough for me; they can't be any worse."

Cheerful crusaders are cheerful lovers of humanity—sinners and saints alike. They relate to the human race as if they were part of it.

Resources for Discussion

1. The author says that an inability to laugh at human foibles is blasphemy. These are strong words. What does he mean? Do you agree?
2. How does laughing at our own foul-ups bring relief? How is it a form of confession?
3. Laughing at our most deeply held concerns, the author says, enables us to avoid "idolatry of the cause." What does he mean? Doesn't lightheartedness result in reducing our passion for a cause?
4. This chapter pokes fun at several concerns—feminism, temperance, pacifism, ecology, and the Moral Majority. Examine your own reaction to the jokes about these issues. Did you enjoy the jokes about somebody else's concern more than those about your own? When you read a satire making fun of an issue in which you believe or see a cartoon mocking an event you favor, are you able to laugh? If a person who agrees with a cause tells a joke that pokes fun at it, how does that affect your reaction?
5. Thoreau said, "If a man has a pain in his bowels, he forthwith sets about reforming the world." Is it possible to commit oneself to important social reforms without a grim disposition? Can we save the world and laugh about it at the same time?
6. Think about a serious cause in which you've involved yourself. Are you and your colleagues able to laugh at yourselves and your crusade in the middle of the battle? Or is the intensity of the concern too great for self-deprecating laughter?

PART TWO

HUMOR HURTS

A familiar comedy routine features a soldier who is "mortally" wounded by six arrows in his chest, three in his back, and one in the middle of his forehead. A companion kneels beside him and asks, "Does it hurt?" In a rasping voice he replies, "Only when I laugh."

It hurts to be the target of laughter. Some humor is intended to wound others, and we can use it as a deliberate act of hostility. We can use hurtful humor as a prophetic instrument—exposing wickedness and hypocrisy. Or we can use jokes that ridicule persons and mock groups simply because we're insensitive. To the recipient, however, the motive matters not. Whether it comes from meanies or crusaders or clods, the laughter still bites and bruises.

Christians need to be aware of the hurting powers of humor. It can be a weapon in noble efforts to right wrongs, but it can also be a force in ignoble attempts to wrong rights.

If conditions for trust and intimacy are not present, sexist jokes hurt women, and racist humor, at best, produces nervous laughter. There is such a creature as a clean joke about sex, but there is also a legion of dirty stories which demean and degrade human sexuality. What we find funny sometimes reveals the dark corners of our souls.

I've argued that humorous laughter is its own excuse for being, and I stand by that. But it's also a means for hurting others, and it should be used exactly the same way a porcupine sleeps on an air mattress—very carefully.

6

Goring Their Ox

During the war in Vietnam, columnist Art Buchwald regularly satirized the military effort there. He
ridiculed official communiqués that announced "we
had to destroy the village in order to save it." He
parodied the never-fulfilled promises that there was
"light at the end of the tunnel." Those in high
places, such as presidents, were used to criticism of
their policies, but they found it difficult to respond
to Buchwald's biting humor.

Buchwald, in an interview, commented on President Johnson's reaction to his columns. He said:
"Some of my inside sources tell me that President
Johnson reads me and chuckles. Other equally in-
formed sources tell me that he does not read me. I
suspect that the truth lies somewhere in between: he
reads me but does not chuckle."

HUMOR HURTS

Humor is a powerful weapon, and it can be used as a tool to make prophetic statements. Jeremiah wore a yoke around his neck to symbolize Judah's coming captivity, and Ezekiel ate a scroll to emphasize his having internalized God's word of judgment. Political cartoonists and many humorous writers approach the prophetic task somewhat differently, but they provoke reactions exactly like those prophets received. We may laugh or we may respond in rage, but probably we will not do both.

Which we do—chuckle or gnash our teeth—depends on whether our ox is being gored. A cartoon by Herblock can generate more "amens" or cries of "foul" than a hundred solemn editorials. When an ox has been gored by a humorous statement, the gore-ee cries out in indignation—and finds nothing funny about the statement.

Gary Trudeau's *Doonesbury* comic strip has prompted both cheers and jeers from its readers for its sharp satire about political figures and events. In fact, some newspaper publishers moved it from the comics to the editorial page because so many subscribers protested its presence in the "funnies." ("The Doonesbury comic strip is in no sense a comic strip. Going over the past six months of this strip I find nothing funny about it and I believe it would be in the best interest of your readers not to renew this strip when renewal time comes around.") Take that, Doonesbury! The person who wrote the letter undoubtedly disagreed with the political stance the cartoonist took in the comic strip. Hence, he could not receive it in an attitude of fun. Nor was it intended to make anyone laugh who disagreed with the cartoonist's point of view. The intent was to gore an ox, and humor was the weapon.

Goring Their Ox

Similar reactions came when a Charles Werner cartoon appeared shortly after Sandra O'Connor was appointed to the Supreme Court. The drawing pictured eight gavels and one rolling pin on the justices' bench. The cartoon generated a deluge of responses, most of them negative. One letter in particular illustrates how offended a recipient of barbed humor can feel.

> Perhaps [the Werner cartoon] meant to state that, in the cartoonist's and the editor's opinion, it is impossible for Sandra O'Connor to base her judicial decisions on anything other than her female experience, that by placing a woman on the Supreme Court we risk impairing impartiality in upholding the law of the land.

> An excellent test of whether . . . the paper oversteps the bounds of discrimination and taste . . . would be to substitute an obviously offensive racist prop. If the president's nominee had been a black male, would you have published the cartoon showing neatly aligned gavels and one, say, watermelon?

The writers of that letter were, as the King James Version might have put it, tick-ethed off. We do not know for sure whether or not the cartoonist was against, on principle, the nomination of a woman to the Supreme Court. If he was, his point was perfectly understood by the letter writers. If he was trying merely to be cute, he made a mistake. The feelings that a comic statement about a controversial idea can generate run deep. Barbed humor leaves recipients feeling vulnerable, victimized, and helpless. Good and mad is what it leaves them! Sticks and stones may break our bones, but spoofing our beliefs is as funny as water to a drowning man.

61

Indeed, the power of humor to gore, to rankle, or to make a prophetic statement as loudly as Amos did is obvious. Caricature attacks persons and positions, and whether the injured parties are justly or unjustly accused, they still react to the pain. At the turn of the century, a Pennsylvania governor drafted a bill prohibiting "the depicting of men . . . as birds or animals" after seeing himself sketched as a rotund parrot. Philadelphia cartoonists responded by drawing well-known political figures as vegetables!

Thomas Nast, a cartoonist before the turn of the century, invented such enduring images as the Democratic donkey and the Republican elephant. He was also instrumental in turning the infamous "Boss Tweed" out of office. Five years of Nast's cartoons depicted Tweed as a haughty Roman emperor or a vulture preying on the populace. There was nothing funny about Nast's attack. Entertainment was a distant second to the use of a cartoon as a weapon.

Mark Twain used a religious context to make a satirical attack on war. Samuel Clemens refused to allow his "Unspoken War Prayer" to be published until after his death because he said, "I have told the whole truth in that, and only dead men can tell the truth in this world":

Oh, Lord our Father, our young patriots, idols of our hearts, go forth to battle. Be Thou near them! With them—in spirit—we also go from the sweet peace of our beloved firesides to smite the foe.

Oh, Lord, our God, help us to tear their soldiers to bloody shreds with our shells; help us to cover their smiling fields with the pale forms of their patriot dead; help us to drown the thunder of the guns with the wounded, writhing in pain; help us to lay waste their humble homes with the hurricane of fire; help us to wring the hearts of their unoffending widows with unavailing grief; help us to turn them out roofless with their little children to wander unfriended over wastes of their desolated land in rags and hunger and thirst, sport of the sun-flames of summer and the icy winds of winter, broken in spirit, worn with travail, imploring Thee for the refuge of the grave and denied it—for our sakes, who adore Thee, Lord, blast their hopes, blight their lives, protract their bitter pilgrimage, make heavy their steps, water their way with their tears, stain the white snow with the blood of their wounded feet! We ask of One who is the spirit of Love and who is the ever faithful refuge and friend of all that are sore beset, and seek His aid with humble and contrite hearts. Grant our prayer, oh Lord, and Thine shall be the praise and honor and glory, now and ever. Amen.[1]

Other comic prophets have been less abrasive than Nast or Twain, possibly because their crusades were less focused and dealt with small sins. Will Rogers was famous for political commentary. He once said: "I guess I wouldn't be very humorous if it weren't for government. I don't make jokes; I just watch the government and report the facts."

Aristophanes, it was said, was the only poet who had the nerve to tell the truth to the Athenians. And telling the truth to politicians and bureaucrats is never a guarantee of a long life and full pension. In dictatorships and authoritarian governments there is steadfast refusal by leaders either to laugh at themselves or to allow the public to laugh at them. In totalitarian countries, for example, any humorous satire directed at official programs borders on treason.

Jokes about the government have been literally smuggled out of Hungary and Russia. In East Germany where government restriction of organized religion is well known, there exists an underground of jokes about the official atheist stance. An example, collected before the death of Russian Communist Party chief Leonid Breshnev: Two border guards, an East German and a West German, arrived at their checkpoints, which were only a few feet apart. The West German said, "It's almost time to go off duty. Thank God." The East German said, "It's almost time to go off duty. Thank Breshnev."

To this, the West German replied, "But what will you say when Breshnev is dead?"

The East German answered, "Thank God."

"It was one of the redeeming features of ancient and medieval monarchies," writes Conrad Hyers, "to have recognized that every king needs a court jester, a part of whose function it is not only to make the king laugh but to make him laugh at himself. In the grotesque form of the jester, the king in all his pompous authority and power is revealed to his courtiers and to himself as also something of a clown."[2]

Christians, by and large, have seldom chosen the role of the jester in their efforts to confront powers and principalities. They have preferred a frontal, direct attack when called to speak a prophetic word. Righteous indignation seldom appears in joking form. So Christians have resorted to the sermon, the editorial, or the angry pronouncement.

Too bad. Big sins and small ones deserve the hardest blows we can manage, and laughing at political stupidity and satirizing injustice are at least as effective as outrage. "Boss Tweed's" political power depended upon the support of a large immigrant population, many of whom could not read or write. Therefore, he ignored what the newpapers wrote about him and what preachers said about him in sermons. But Nast's cartoons infuriated him. Those "damn pictures" had to stop. They were running him out of office. The power of the joke turned out to be mightier than either the sword or the pen.

Humor may be our best weapon for certain kinds of injustice. It can expose corruption and discrimination for what they are—jokes against humanity.

Resources for Discussion

1. The author says humor is often used not to entertain, but as a weapon. Are there political cartoonists or satirists who "gore your ox"? When you react negatively, is it because the spoof or caricature seems unfair?

2. Consider the following jokes about the government. Do you find them funny? Do they cause you to cry "foul"?

    (a) Congress favors a stable government, judging from the amount of stalling it does.

    (b) The business of government is to keep the government out of business—that is, unless business needs government aid (Will Rogers).

    (c) Some people would rather be right than President, while politicians are not so particular.

    (d) Next to handshakings, nothing has been so overworked and successful as promising to reduce taxes (Ken Hubbard).

3. Now change the above jokes slightly and make them personal.

    (a) Congressman (insert name) favors a stable government, judging from the amount of stalling (he, she) does.

    (b) The business of (this administration) is to keep government out of business—unless (name of corporation) needs government aid.

    (c) Some people would rather be right than President, while (Gerald Ford? Lyndon Johnson?) was not so particular.

(d) Next to handshakings, nothing has been so overworked and successful for (Jimmy Carter? Ronald Reagan?) as promising to reduce taxes.

How were your responses affected by changing the jokes from *general* to *specific* situations?

4. Are Christians called to be "court jesters" today? What injustices or excesses can you identify today that deserve to be mocked? What are the advantages of attacking problems with humor rather than with righteous indignation?

5. Examine the cartoon about rape printed below. Is it fair? Is it as effective as, say, an editorial?

"Now, honey, tell us again about this alleged rape."

Betty Swords

7

When Is a Joke Dirty?

The movie was funny and well performed. The actors were skilled, and the script was full of comical situations and witty one-liners. The audience laughed in all the right places. One message of the movie was unmistakable—regular, systematic adultery is worth doing and lots of fun.

Same Time Next Year starred, in the movie version, Alan Alda and Ellen Burstyn. It had had a long, successful run on the stage, and many local companies had performed it in summer stock and amateur productions. It was billed as a comedy, and it was.

It also illustrates why Christians get uptight about humor. They recognize its power to change values, to make acceptable that which is unacceptable if presented in a serious, direct manner. Had a serious essay, entitled "The Case for Adultery," been written, it would have been dealt with openly and un-compromisingly. Set in the context of comedy, how-ever, the rules change. Those who deny adultery as appropriate are put on the defensive.

"C'mon, it was just a funny play. I'll bet you laughed, too."

Many of us who disapprove of adultery for relig-ious, moral, psychological, and sociological reasons laugh aloud and set aside our objections. Humor is disarming. Its power to unite people, break down prejudices, and transform unpleasant things into tol-erable ones can also change values. If we laugh hard enough and long enough at jokes that deny our be-liefs, one day we discover the beliefs themselves have lost their power. Hollywood movies and television sitcoms have done this with America's sexual mores. And comedy has played a significant part in the de-valuation process.

"Three's Company" has been a popular show on television for years. Its humor is largely based on sexual innuendo, tolerance for irresponsible sexual activity, and female sexual stereotypes. It is too stupid to be taken seriously, hence its contribution to the erosion of responsible sexuality has gone largely unchallenged.

The movie, *Porky's,* was billed as a hilarious ac-count of growing up. One reviewer said "it poked fun at the typical complexities of passing through adolescence." Those "typical complexities" featured slapstick comedy based on voyeurism, prostitution, and nymphomania. Why get upset over jokes about the normal, fun-loving process of growing up?

At this writing two of the country's most popular entertainers, Burt Reynolds and Dolly Parton, are starring in still another side-splitting comedy, based on another popular play, with the subtle title, *The Best Little Whorehouse in Texas.* No doubt it will earn its producers lots of money and help intimidate all of us narrow-minded types who oppose prostitution.

The night our family, including Ruthie, age twelve, went to see *Meatballs,* we expected to see a funny story about the antics of a crazy summer camp. That's what the ads promised. They were partly right, for there were several funny scenes, such as one in which the camp director, a sound sleeper, was floated out to the middle of the lake on a raft. Worked into the movie, however, was the annual staff drinking bout and friendly orgy. And it ended on a high note, as the lovable, bumbling director and the ever-patient heroine decide to live together.

Etc. Etc. Etc.

Sex as a theme of humor has been around forever. (What did Eve say the first night she and Adam were together? "Sorry, Adam, I've got a headache.") Granted, also, religious fears of sex have sometimes been extreme and occasionally as obscene as a dirty joke. However, those who think our current problem in movies, television, books, and plays is that of sexual puritanism have either been in a coma or were brought up by werewolves.

Tweren't always so. For good reasons and bad, there was a time when public risqué humor was risky. Before 1950, about as far as any radio program dared to go was a Fred Allen comment that Admiral Byrd's dog went crazy looking for the South Pole. That joke, obviously, is more seriously judged by taste than morality and is essentially harmless.

Humor that *changes* sexual norms (for example, that which implies adultery is acceptable) is a different matter.

There is such a creature as the clean sexual joke. Our task is to decide which jokes are funny because they are true and fair, and which ones don't qualify because they violate values which are important. Sex has no innate connection with laughter. It is, obviously, of unflagging interest to the human race and has a way of bursting into our minds on the slightest provocation. Freud was right in believing that jokes are often release from adult inhibitions, and jokes about sex can be healthy outlets. It's like saying, "If Christians aren't supposed to have sex before marriage or commit adultery after marriage, may we laugh about it occasionally along the way?" A good question.

Here is a test case: A woman got on a train with nine children, and when the conductor came for her tickets, the woman said, "Now these three are thirteen years old and pay full fare, but these three over there are only six, and these three here are four and a half." The conductor looked at her in astonishment.

"Do you mean to say you get three every time?" he asked.

"Oh, no," she replied. "Sometimes we don't get any at all."

Is this a clean or dirty joke? (My daughter found it merely unfunny). *The Wittenburg Door,* a Christian humor magazine (some question whether it is Christian, others whether it is humorous) tried to provide standards for judging jokes about sex. Ben Patterson, the editor, suggested the following:

When Is a Joke Dirty?

I'm going to say arbitrarily that a joke is dirty if it debases God's good gift of sex. Humor that leers, obscures, or degrades is sinful. . . . Can there be clean humor about sex? I think so. It is clean if it in some way illumines or places sex in its proper perspective. Unlike dirty humor, whose source is basically hostile and destructive, clean humor proceeds from a basically friendly and constructive attitude.

Sex has always made extravagant claims for itself. Depending on whom you listen to, it can send you to heaven or hell. Both are extravagant claims, and both are false. "Contrary to Mrs. Grundy, sex is not sin," says Frederick Buechner. "Contrary to Hugh Hefner, it's not salvation either." Sex is sex. It is human, nothing more and nothing less.[1]

Patterson raises an interesting point. How do we determine what is a "basically friendly and constructive attitude"? What kind of humor about sex is free of claims to be either sin or salvation? Like an ink blot test, a joke that causes "sin" or promises "salvation" for one will do neither for another.

In my own upbringing, sex as a general subject was simply avoided. While jokes were a mainstay of our family life, jokes about sex were taboo. When my grandmother who lived with us did the laundry, she hung the underwear inside the pillowcases to dry. One does not grow up under such circumstances and freely accept all kinds of sexual humor.

Some of us can laugh about sexual jokes set in the context of marriage that would leave us uneasy if told about unmarried teenagers. Sexual jokes that use obscene language also damage the "fun" of their humor for many people. Consider this old joke:

The bride and groom were riding in a car on the way to their honeymoon cottage. The engine malfunctioned, and the car came puffing to a stop. The couple, who believed in equal marriage, got out and both crawled under the car to fix it. After awhile a policeman tapped them on the shoulder and said, "Begging your pardon, did you know your car had been stolen?"

Would this story have been "dirty" if told about two teenagers? Had it been explicit in detail, would it have crossed a line that made it unfriendly and destructive?

If we ask too many questions, of course, any joke—clean or dirty—ceases to be funny. If we ask no questions, on the other hand, the line is regularly crossed, and irresponsible sexual attitudes are taken for granted.

Those persons who have been happily married for many years know that sex is the most fun you can have without laughing. Sex is worth laughing about—worth the risk of occasional poor taste, worth even the wrath of those for whom sex will never be a joke.

One of the lesser-known prophets, W. C. Fields, said; "Some things are better than sex, and some things are worse, but there's nothing exactly like it." A paraphrase also contains truth: "Some things are funnier than sex, and some things aren't, but there's nothing as funny in quite the same way."

Resources for Discussion

1. Do you agree with the point that comedy has played a significant part in the devaluation of sexual standards? (Mullen cites television sitcoms and "funny" movies as examples.) Is he taking such presentations too seriously in terms of their power to bring about change?"

2. Is there such a thing as a clean joke about sex? What is your reaction to the story about the woman with nine children? Would the story about the bride and groom crawling under the car have been less acceptable if it had been told about two teenagers?

3. In a discussion about the movie, *Same Time Next Year,* one participant said the story was not really about adultery but the poignancy of human relationships. He argues that it had deeper meaning that went above and beyond the surface account of two people who annually met to commit adultery. If we are *sophisticated* enough, will we be able to laugh at, say, adulterous goings-on because we are not trapped by the obvious?

4. Many jokes are clearly dirty because of their obscene language and demeaning content. Others are not so easily evaluated. Ben Patterson's criteria for deciding whether jokes are clean or dirty can be summarized as follows:

   (a) Jokes are dirty if they *debase* sex. Humor that *leers, obscures,* or *degrades* is sinful.

(b) Jokes are clean if they put sex in a proper perspective. Clean humor proceeds from a basically friendly and constructive attitude.

Using the above as guidelines, how do you evaluate these one-liners?

(a) "The odds are usually two to one in favor of sex: you and she against her conscience."

(b) "There are only two kinds of girls: those that do, and those that are never asked."

(c) "A bikini is like a barbed wire fence: it protects the property without obstructing the view."

(d) "Many a man finds true happiness in marriage, but only because his wife doesn't watch him too closely."

(e) "Prostitution is a game where the man gets a little fun, and the woman gets a little fund."

8

Nervous Laughter

In 1977 Randy Newman wrote a song entitled "Short People." It was about short people having grubby little fingers and dirty little minds. "Got to pick 'em up just to say hello," and so on. By his own testimony Newman meant no offense.

"It's just a joke," he explained when the song was released.

The song was banned by several radio stations and became the subject of three songs in response, each entitled "Tall People." One legislator (5'5" tall) in Maryland proposed a statewide prohibition of the song.

"I don't get why people are so offended by it," Newman said. "It's just a joke. Why are people offended?"

Why, indeed? Because it hurts when we feel *singled* out as the butt of a joke. Short people were offended because to be laughed at was to be picked upon. Polish people get tired of being treated in stories as if they were stupid clods, so Polish-American organizations in Chicago and Milwaukee printed newspaper protests, releasing long-contained anger at ethnic humor. Women have stopped "going along" with men who tell sexist jokes.

When we are *laughed at* again and again, the humor dies. Public humor does not have the close relationship that allows racist, ethnic, or sexist jokes to be acceptable. People wonder, "Does the joke teller *really* think we Polish are all stupid?" Or, "Does he *really* think we women are as incompetent or silly as sexist jokes make us out to be?"

Humor has been a mechanism down through the years for practicing racism and sexism. All one needs to do to be convinced of this is to read the jokes in old issues of *The Reader's Digest* or *Saturday Evening Post* in which anecdotes with racial and sexist stereotypes abound.

Chris Mullins, a staff writer for the *Kansas City Times,* probably spoke for many of her readers when she vented her anger in a column titled, "The Senator's Little Joke Was Not Kind of Funny."[1]

> State Senator John Vermillion of Independence, Kansas, believes that "what women really like to do is put on a pair of high heels and strut their stuff."
> Stick it in your ear, Senator. . . .
> Some of my men friends asked me if I didn't really think the remark was, well, kind of funny.
> I said I failed to see the humor in it. They said they failed to see why I couldn't. That's what's wrong with the women's movement, they said, dolefully shaking their heads—can't take a joke.

Horsefeathers. . . . I'm quite capable of laughing at myself [but] Senator Vermillion's remark is not funny because it lacks the critical element of humor—truth. Somewhere, buried in the jabs and jibes and schtick, must be that pinpoint, dead-on accuracy that stings us into nodding our heads and admitting, if somewhat sheepishly, "Ain't it the truth."

She goes on to say that men, too, "strut their stuff" by dress and manner, and the condition is not peculiar to women. Hence, she argues, the remark was untrue and therefore unfunny.

Jokes that build unflattering stereotypes are seldom "kinda funny." They sometimes are used consciously to keep persons or groups in their place. In cruel laughter we exclude certain persons. "All Indians walk in single file. At least the only one I ever saw did." That's not fair to Indians mainly because it simply isn't true.

For example, the following one-liner deals with a familiar female stereotype—women as poor drivers.

If a woman driver ahead of you signals a left turn, be very careful. She may turn left.

When told to a group of seminary women, that joke produced almost as much laughter as a public execution. Their response was proper because (1) it referred to women in general, not a particular person whose reputation as a crazy driver might have been deserved; and (2) it was based on an untruth, namely, that women are worse drivers than men. At least, insurance companies know it to be untrue; their rates are lower for new women drivers than for new men drivers.

Poor driving, however, is a fit topic for jokes:

A woman driver is a person who drives the same way a man does, only she gets blamed for it.

This is a better one-liner because it pokes fun at both men and women and at sloppy driving in general.

When we are sensitive to the hurting power of humor, we begin to filter our anecdotes and stories. Instead of thinking, "Why can't women *like that* take a joke?" we can put ourselves into a comparable position of vulnerability. Lawyers weary of jokes about their dishonesty and lack of ethics—their ambulance-chasing image. ("Lawyers will sometimes tell the truth. They will do anything to win a case.") Physicians laugh less heartily than their patients at stories about their wealth, arrogance, and unwillingness to make house calls. ("Nature cures but doctors send the bill.")

Ministers grin and force chuckles when they are victims, for the hundredth time, of jokes about boring sermons or working only one day a week. ("A minister is a person who is invisible for six days and incomprehensible on the seventh.") Author's note: An effective reply to those who kid about working only one day a week is this: "Yes, it's true we work only one day a week, but do you realize that when we get two weeks vacation, we're really getting only two days?"

The truth test applies in all the instances above. More ministers err on the side of being workaholics than being lazy. Polls reveal that, while the public regards physicians as less-caring and more money-hungry than they once did, they also have high regard for *their* doctors. And *their* attorneys.

Because professional people are a part of the mainstream of society—and know it—doctors, lawyers, and ministers will suffer less pain from jokes at their expense than, say, minority groups. Racist humor has been used to keep people down—to keep them, as it were, in their place. J. H. Burma, a sociologist, was the first to deal systematically with the social functions of humor in race relations, and he concluded that jokes have long been a vehicle for "conveying malice." "Racial humor is primarily created to attain gratification at the expense of the other racial group; its purpose is to cause one's adversary to appear ludicrous in his own eyes or in your eyes."[2]

Racial humor sometimes backfires. Public figures have been penalized for remarks that revealed prejudice, and then all were reminded how hurtful racial comments can be. G. Harold Carswell was denied confirmation to the United States Supreme Court for several reasons, not the least of which was his telling a racist joke in public. Earl Butz, former Secretary of Agriculture, was removed from office because of his racist-sexual joke was regarded as symptomatic of a basic attitude.

Racist humor fails the acceptability test on two counts—its stereotypes of Blacks as lazy and ignorant are untrue, and such jokes are seldom told in a spirit of fun and charity. Tellers of racist jokes are sometimes innocent of bad motives but guilty of poor taste, that is, insensitivity. Those seeking to be Christian, even in their joking, are properly directed to the Sermon on the Mount, in which both *intention* and *action* are standards.

The problem of racist and ethnic jokes, however, will not be solved simply by better selection of material and an audience poll to determine what offends and what does not. Most studies of the social effects of humor indicate that the more secure a group feels about itself and its place in society, the more able it is to deal with jokes at its own expense. Middle-class Blacks are freer to laugh at racial jokes than poor Blacks who are conscious of being put down regularly. Jewish humor about Jewish people became public after Jews felt more at home in American culture.

So, if a serious plea for justice is not sufficient by itself, we can add one more reason to work for equality, brotherhood, and fair play. Perhaps when the day comes that the lion and the lamb lie down peacefully together, the scene will be characterized by rolling tides of laughter. When lions and lambs become brothers and sisters in God's family, they'll be "in fun" together.

Until then, the lamb may have to laugh at the lion's joke—very nervously.

Resources for Discussion

1. Why do ethnic jokes remain popular? Is it because we need scapegoats or groups about whom we can feel superior? Who are the groups who are the butt of jokes in your community? Blacks? Indians? Poles? Jews? Appalachians? Newfoundlanders? (Note: The jokes remain the same. The ethnic groups are interchangeable.)
2. Here are four jokes about women. Do you find them funny? Do they pass the truth test?

    (a) Angry wife to husband: "No! Everytime we discuss something sensibly, I lose!"
    (b) The women's liberation movement has liberated some women from hats, shoes, stockings, slips, and bras. The next thing you know, they'll be complaining because they have nothing to wear.
    (c) Spokesperson for matronly threesome to cab driver: "Would you mind driving another ten cents' worth? Three just won't go into four dollars and ten cents evenly."
    (d) Woman after head-on collision with male motorist: "You had no right to assume that I had made up my mind!"

    Can these jokes be modified so that they don't depend upon stereotypes for their humor?
3. Do you agree with the sociologist, J. H. Burma, who concluded that jokes have been a vehicle for "conveying malice?" Have you ever been the victim of a joke wherein you felt ridiculed or put

down because you were a woman, a lawyer, an evangelical, a Pole, or something else? How did you respond to the joke-teller at the time it happened?

4. What would you do in this situation? A man is telling a joke about Black people that is racist in tone, that is, it depends upon an imitation of dialect and a stereotype of Negroes as lazy for the punch line. There are six people present, but no Blacks. The others laugh heartily.

9

Hollow Humor

The junior high youth fellowship was over, and its most passionate interest—eating—was being satisfied. Veteran parents that we were, we accepted our proper role, which was to keep the groceries coming as regularly and unobtrusively as possible. Therefore, we were privy to the conversation our daughter and her friends sustained between bites and drinks.

The conversation was punctuated by jokes. It soon became evident that the joking was taking a curious direction. Rapid-fire anecdotes and one-liners were traded with appropriate squeals and groans interspersed:

Question: "What is green and yellow and lies in a ditch with cookie crumbs all over it?"
Answer: "A dead girl scout!"

Question: "Mrs. Jones, may Bobbie come out and play baseball?"

Answer: "Roger, you know that Bobbie doesn't have any arms or legs!"

Response: "Yes, m'am, but we'd like to use him for second base."

Child: "But daddy, I don't want to go to Europe for the summer!"

Father: "Shut up and keep swimming."

Child: "But mother, I don't want to see grandma."

Mother: "Just keep digging!"

The supply of such jokes was inexhaustible. For most in the group, the jokes were familiar, and they laughed the same way we all laugh when reminded of an old story. Such humor has a name—sick—and it is well known to teenagers and young adults across America.

Is it sick? Dead girl scouts, handicapped children, and abusive parents are not the usual subjects for humor. Like cancer, aren't some topics simply taboo, unfit subject matter for jokes?

Psychologizing about the reasons for such humor is not difficult. One does not have to be Sigmund Freud to explain why teenagers—particularly those of junior-high vintage—tell dead baby jokes and make fun of Helen Keller's handicaps. There is, after all, shock value in sick humor, a verbal form of unexpected craziness intended to startle listeners into giggles.

Also, such jokes function as a rite of passage for adolescents. The stories provide (they think) a way of dealing with "adult" topics. Then, too, this particular group of teenagers was aware one of THEM (a parent) was listening, and the jokes may have functioned as a way of defining who was in and out of the group.

Some psychologists speculate, further, that teenagers tell sick jokes as a way of dealing with fear. A violent and cruel world is full of hurtful and frightening events, and telling a joke about them may flush the boogey-person out of the shadows.

Or it may be simply that there wasn't enough stovepipe—no Deeper Meanings, just spontaneous stuff offered while "in fun."

Figuring out why teenagers laugh or cry is, at best, an inexact science. "Sick" jokes help us see, however, that we are able to laugh about almost any subject, whether or not we cross a line into poor taste. They also serve as preface for another point: What we find to be funny can reveal our worst selves, our "heart of darkness," as novelist Joseph Conrad called it.

Both fiction and daily life provide many illustrations of hardhearted laughter. The worst picture of the Roman Empire is captured in raucous crowds laughing and taunting victims of wild beasts in the arena. (Author's note: A cartoon in a Sunday school magazine two thousand years after the event showed lions attacking Christians in an arena. One little boy examining the picture within the cartoon began to cry: "Look, that poor lion doesn't have any Christian!")

Those who watched the television movie, *The Holocaust,* will remember scenes of cruelty heightened and intensified because of the awful laughter of Nazi torturers. Others may remember a scene from another World War II movie, *The Ipcress File,* in which a Gestapo leader walks down a line of helpless Jewish prisoners, calmly shooting them one by one and watching as they fall backward into their graves. At one point, instead of shooting a victim, he fires into the air. The man, expecting in that moment to be killed, instinctively falls into the trench at the sound of the gun. His look of bafflement mixed with terror as he stares up from his grave was a study in horror. It also was the occasion for gales of laughter from the Gestapo chief and his henchmen.

Fiction and daily police reports are not far apart in their accounts of laughter as evidence of deep cruelty. One newspaper story about a multiple rape by a gang of toughs included this statement by the victim: "The worst part was the way they laughed— like what they did was a big joke. And the more I cried, the harder they laughed."

Sadists laugh sadistic laughter. Evil persons smile in the midst of their inhumanity to others.

Christians are not strangers to this truth. The biblical accounts of Christ on the cross include several explicit examples of derision and taunting. The men who guarded Jesus made fun of him and hit him, taunting him to identify, though he was blindfolded, who his attackers were. "The people stood there watching while the Jewish leaders made fun of him: 'He saved others; let him save himself if he is the Messiah whom God has chosen!' The soldiers also made fun of him: they came up to him and offered him cheap wine, and said, 'Save yourself if you are the king of the Jews!'" (Luke 23:35–37, TEV).

None of us finds humor in any of the above illustrations because readers of books like this one seldom participate, even vicariously, in the grossest forms of inhumanity to others. We abhor rape, murder, and crucifixion. The question for us is this: Is humor that *begins* as tasteless or insensitive on a continuum that *ends* in heartlessness? Are sick jokes the seeds of sick attitudes?

It's hard to know. As we've seen, there are gray areas as to what is appropriate in humor (that is, pleasing to God) and what is not. It's difficult to think those teenagers telling sick jokes in our kitchen while gulping brownies and soda pop are the sick adults of tomorrow. The probability is that psychologists are closer to the truth than alarmists who insist we wash their mouths out with soap.

We have also seen that when a trusting, open relationship has been established, and a state of fun exists, humorous topics know few bounds. Were a handicapped person in the midst of the group, no one would have laughed at the suggestion he be used as second base. In fact, no one would have suggested it. So maybe the continuum idea doesn't wash. Cruel laughter and jokes in bad taste may well be two separate matters.

Still, Christians wary of humor have a point to make. St. Ambrose, Robert Barclay, and that stereotyped horde of sour-puss puritans with their reputation for party-pooping were well acquainted with the dark side of human nature. Tragedy plus time can lead to humor. Tragedy without enough time or distance can produce refined cruelty.

The question of proportion is crucial. If the youth group told "sick" jokes every time it met, the practice would say something negative about how healthy the group was. If a society feeds on humor that puts down people already hurting, its poor diet will cause pimples that lead to scars. Laughing *only* at the expense of others is, at best, a vicarious life. And the vicarious life is not worth living. Hollow people laugh hollow laughter.

Thank God for alternatives. Cruel laughter can be drowned out by a Bill Cosby spinning yarns about his boyhood adventures, going to scary movies, and poor Noah getting directions from the Lord on building an ark. One reading of "The Dog That Wouldn't Come Home" by James Thurber will restore our confidence in human nature, tickle our funny bones, and leave us feeling that life isn't evil after all.

To expect all humor to be innocent, warm-hearted, playful, and affectionate, however, is to expect too much. Laughter based only on childhood reminiscences and puppy dogs would be too safe, too tame, and eventually not very funny. Hence our young people—and older folks, too—will risk an occasional "sick" joke. We will, therefore, experience violations of good taste from time to time. And there is within all of us some degree of hostility that may sneak out in our laughter when our guards are down.

That's the way it is with humor. If, however, we are aware of its power to be hateful, we can head off most of the problems at the pass. And if the goodness of life is our steady diet as far as jokes are concerned, we will be able to survive occasional excesses without indigestion.

Laughter for good reasons leads to joy, and it is more fun than laughing to release hostility. Playing competitive games is a better way of getting rid of malevolent feelings than throwing rocks. Therefore, we are well-advised to follow the example of Max

Shulman, who played croquet as an outlet for frustration and anger. "It helps when I play croquet," he said, "because I always play with mallets toward none."

Resources for Discussion

1. Consider the various explanations for sick jokes offered in this chapter: They have "shock" value. They serve as a rite of passage for adolescents. They define a group, or they cover up fears about frightening topics. Are there other reasons why such jokes are popular among young people? Do you think they are harmful? Would you attempt to restrict their usage?

2. There are adult forms of "sick" humor, too. Ridicule is probably the most obvious one. Does what we find funny reveal the dark side of ourselves? Is "sick humor" on a continuum that ends in heartlessness? Are "sick" jokes the seeds of a sick attitude?

3. The author writes: "Tragedy plus time can lead to humor. Tragedy without enough time can produce refined cruelty." What does he mean? Do you agree?

4. Do some people avoid jokes because they have been the butt of them so often? How would you help a person who has been victimized by hateful humor?

5. In terms of *proportion,* how would you grade the condition of today's public humor—that which comes to us via comedians on television, comic strips, movies, and humorous literature? Do you judge a lot of it to be in poor taste or cruel? Do you regard it as mainly stupid? Or do you find most of it fair, inclusive, and playfully poking fun at human foibles? Give examples for your answers.

6. How do we explain the popularity of "funny horror movies?" Students comment that they go to, say, *Friday the 13th* or *Halloween II* to "be scared and to laugh." What is entertaining about the combination of humor and horror?

PART THREE

HUMOR HEALS

Humor is worth its risks because laughter has healing properties. Christian people try not to hurt others, and therefore some of them avoid jokes and stories altogether. A completely sober perspective, they think, will prevent their doing harm to others.

Not so. When we fail to laugh at a child's antics which are intended to entertain, we deliver a negative message. Furthermore, nurturing laughter in our homes is at least equal in importance to teaching responsibility or how to pray.

Humorous laughter is directly connected to good health. It is a survival mechanism, too, enabling us to forgive and remember what we can't forgive and forget. The ability to laugh in a world like ours is an act of faith, a declaration of belief in a God who can be trusted.

Humorous laughter in the face of tragedy depends upon an intimate relationship with God. It is like being "in fun" with the Creator. Psalm 2:4 says that "he that sitteth in the heavens shall laugh." Some commentators say that God's laughter in this passage is derision; others think it means good-humored laughter. Either way, to laugh with God is to see life for what it is—full of foibles but ultimately worth living.

So God sits in the heavens and laughs. That's worth noting, for the Creator, after all, has the best seat in the house.

10

Medicine and Merry Hearts

Humorous laughter can be an agent of physical healing. Norman Cousins, former editor of *The Saturday Review*, prescribed his own treatment for a life-threatening illness, and his regimen for recovery included deliberately using humor as treatment.[1]

Cousins discovered he had a serious collagen disease. Collagen is a substance, found in the connective tissue of the body, which holds the cells and larger structures of the body together. Because of his illness, Cousins experienced great difficulty and pain in moving his joints, and medical specialists held out little hope for recovery.

Cousins, however, had read of the role of the endocrine system in fighting disease and of the adverse consequences *negative* emotional states had on the chemical balance of the body. He concluded that positive emotions could compensate for negative emotions that had made him sick in the first place.

Therefore, he took charge of his own case. He watched funny television clips—specifically, some old *Candid Camera* segments—and noted that laughter was a powerful analgesic. One ten-minute interlude of laughter yielded two hours of painless sleep. Inflammation also was significantly reduced after each session of laughter.

Norman Cousins might have recovered anyway, without the laughter. Since his case is unusual, it does not represent a scientific breakthrough. Even so, it is important to note that Cousins is an intellectual's intellectual. He is a rational person far removed in perspective from, say, Oral Roberts. Yet he is convinced that laughter was a key to his healing.

He is not alone in that belief. Raymond A. Moody, Jr., a physician, wrote *Laugh after Laugh: The Healing Power of Humor* because of his interest in how laughter and humor relate to health and disease. He argues that laughter and a sense of humor are healing assets usually overlooked.

Moody, for example, shows how clowns have been able to bring people back from severely withdrawn and unresponsive states—even after medical efforts have failed. Two cases illustrate his point:

> One clown ... related how, as he was walking through a large hospital, he saw a little girl with a doll of his likeness lying beside her as she was being fed by a nurse. As the clown walked in, the child said his name, whereupon the nurse threw down the spoon and dashed off to call the physician. For the child—diagnosed as catatonic—had been unresponsive for six months. The doctor was able to get her to

follow up this first communication with other responses, and the child progressively improved following this breakthrough.

In another case, a ninety-five-year-old man was admitted to the hospital with severe depression. He had not eaten for several days and for the same period had not said a word to anyone. His physicians were alarmed; they were concerned that he would soon die. A clown entered his hospital room and within thirty minutes had succeeded in getting the elderly man to talk, to laugh, and to eat.[2]

A sense of humor has been connected with longevity, too. Those who laugh often, tradition says, live long. Specialists in gerontology have observed that healthy, very elderly patients invariably demonstrate a spirit of fun. One gerontologist commented that the stereotype of old people as grumpy is a myth. Some old people are, indeed, grumpy but they probably were grumpy when they were young. In fact, this specialist concluded, "If people are too grouchy too long, they don't get old. They die."

Her comment illustrates another way in which a humorous perspective has healing qualities. Humor is more than diversion. Laughing does not merely take our minds off the aches and pains of getting older. It reminds us that good health, at best, lasts only a lifetime. Having a humorous perspective means having an attitude toward aging that accepts getting older and demonstrates that acceptance by being able to laugh about the process.

A man who wrote to Ann Landers demonstrated this attitude:

HUMOR HEALS

Dear Ann Landers:

You know you are getting older when:

Almost everything hurts. What doesn't hurt, doesn't work anymore.

It feels like the morning after the night before, and you haven't been anywhere.

All the names in your little black book end in M.D.

You get winded playing chess.

You look forward to a dull evening.

You still chase women but have forgotten why.

You turn out the lights for economic, not romantic, reasons.

Your knees buckle and your belt won't.

You are 17 around the neck, 42 around the waist, and 126 around the golf course.

You sink your teeth into a steak and they stay there.

You try to straighten the wrinkles in your socks and find you aren't wearing any.

A little old gray-haired lady tries to help you across the street. She's your wife.

Perspective about aging, of course, comes more easily when we have not had to face certain kinds of pain and tragedy getting older can bring. Yet, as one pundit put it, aging is not so bad when you consider the alternative. Laughing is surely a healthier response than attempts to deny growing old by cosmetics, surgery, and false this-and-thats. A humorous perspective frees people from the fear of it being "found out" that they're no longer young. When our girdle pops or we forget the name of the best man at our wedding, we can join in the fun and laugh *with* those who notice.

The ability to laugh even in the face of disfigurement, blindness, or other serious handicap is remarkable in its effects, both for handicapped persons and those close to them.

Examples of persons laughing in the midst of their own pain and handicaps are several but by no means universal. Indeed, the contrast between, say, a blind person whose life is infected by laughter and one whose life is tainted by bitterness makes the point. The difference is not the fact of blindness; it is the way a sense of humor provides a healthy acceptance of the handicap.

I knew one blind woman, remarkable for her independence and self-sufficiency, who continually freed others to accept her handicap for, as she put it, "what it was—a major inconvenience." Her cheerful spirit manifested itself again and again in her ability to laugh at the unlaughable—her own blindness. On one occasion she was scheduled to attend a meeting, and a friend volunteered to give her a ride. The blind woman accepted and then remarked, "Remember, if you arrive and all the lights are out, that doesn't mean I've already left."

A sense of humor is developed along the way. When a person faces a crippling illness, it helps little to say, "Now, you'll have to learn how to laugh about it." Indeed, the laughter will necessarily have to come from within the person and cannot be demanded or urged by those outside the problem. That's why cultivating the ability to be "in fun" during childhood is important. It's why the capacity for laughter at one's self *before* a crisis arrives is preventive medicine.

Humor and hypochondria are natural enemies. Hypochondriacs go through life on their deathbeds, but a sense of humor enables us to accept life, bruises and all. Humor helps define the line which divides reasonable care of ourselves from nervous preoccupation with the care and feeding of our bodies.

Laughing in the midst of illness is not easy. Anyone who has spent time as a patient in a hospital knows the temptation to wallow in self-pity and whine for sympathy. I learned this lesson experientially the first time I had surgery.

My aim was to go through it cheerfully and courageously, smiling through the pain and providing a high moral example to family and friends. The surgery itself—a hemorrhoidectomy—did not lend itself to such goals. Actually, it hurt a lot and didn't seem very funny. The inner desire was for sympathy and concern. Courage was still in order, but whimpering, not joking, came naturally.

For better or worse, however, hemmorrhoid surgery does not produce outpourings of sympathy, particularly from those who have not experienced it. Family and friends try, but there is something about an operation on the bottom that provokes laughter and bad jokes. My own brother, a minister who regularly visits sick people in hospitals, did not send a get-well card. Instead, his miserable, suffering brother opened his mail to find a card with this message: "Do you know what Eskimos who sit around their igloos all day get?" Answer: Polaroids!

Nor could the Dean of the school where I teach resist. A nice note containing wishes for a speedy recovery concluded: "I know you're glad that's all behind you now!" A hemorrhoidectomy patient is the butt of his own joke.

Laughter is not denial of pain. Joking in the middle of suffering indicates neither masochism on the part of the sufferer nor sadism on the part of others. Done "in fun" and in the context of a caring relationship, such laughter provides us with an attitude of gratitude for life itself.

Proverbs 17:22 is right: "A merry heart doeth good like a medicine: but a broken spirit drieth the bones."

Resources for Discussion

1. Do you share the belief that a sense of humor (a playful disposition) has a positive influence on health? Consider the two cases quoted from Moody's book, *Laugh After Laugh*. Do they seem far-fetched?
2. Does a playful disposition result in good health, or does good health enable us to have a playful disposition? Among people you know, do you find a connection between humor and their health?
3. Does laughing about one's infirmities yield positive effects, or do you think it merely hides a sense of pain and loss? Think of a handicapped person you know. What place does humor play in that individual's attitude and ability to cope with the problem?
4. The author suggests we learn to laugh along the way, for trying to smile bravely through pain *without* having nurtured a playful disposition is nearly impossible. How do we nurture a playful disposition? How do we do it with children? If you have a sense of humor, how was it acquired? Can it be learned? Does identifying others who demonstrate an ability to laugh in the face of handicaps encourage others to do the same, or does it hinder another person?
5. Counselors warn against the temptation to cheer up patients we visit who are sick and depressed. They advise us to listen and encourage patients to express pain and loss, not to cover it up with

phony humor. When is humor helpful in relating to a hurting person? Has humor proved helpful to you when faced with surgery or other grim potentialities?

6. Clowns often comment on an exhilarating feeling of freedom from customary social restraints they experience while playing their role in costume. To the degree that a person behaves like a clown, will he or she be liberated from shyness, depression, or feelings of inferiority? What do you think?

11

Healing Memories

Sometime in the last century a prominent European physician was examining an elderly man. After checking him over and listening to his many vague complaints, the physician could find nothing wrong which would account for the patient's symptoms. We might imagine that it occurred to the doctor, just as it might to one of his latter-day colleagues, that his patient's physical complaints were in all probability serving as a mask for deep-seated emotional stress and depression. Suddenly, an inspired idea came to him. It happened that Joseph Grimaldi, perhaps the greatest clown of all time, was in town for a performance that very evening. The physician shrugged his shoulders about his inability to arrive at a diagnosis and suggested to the patient, "Why don't you go to see Grimaldi tonight?" A distressed and disappointed expression suddenly played across the old man's face, and he exclaimed, "Oh, but you don't understand. I am Grimaldi!"[1]

The connection between laughter and sorrow is obvious. Most of us, not just professional clowns, have laughed on the outside while crying on the inside. Many of us use humor as a social lubricant to help us over bad spots in our lives. Elton Trueblood says: "Far from laughter being incompatible with anguish, it is often the natural expression of deep pain."[2]

While jokes can be a cover-up for repressed sorrow or disappointment, humor does other important work when it comes to emotional pain—it can provide genuine healing of memories. A sense of humor and the perspective it eventually provides enables us to be our own therapists. We survive painful or frustrating events, both major and minor, and months or years later we are the life of the party as we recount them for others. Time and a sense of humor transforms them into anecdotes, and healing occurs.

One area wherein this can be observed clearly is in the mixture of frustration and excitement called "parenting." Erma Bombeck describes with hilarious accuracy the state of near-madness raising children can bring. Vicariously, we identify with her words, and this enables us to look at our family experiences in a new light. The next thing we know, we are telling *our* story about the time our three-year-old painted the dog green—even though, then, the incident was decidedly unfunny, particularly to the dog.

Our second daughter, Martha, was the kind of child who regularly managed to spill her milk—sometimes twice a day, although it may have happened more frequently. I wrote a book whose title, *Where 2 or 3 Are Gathered Together, Someone Spills His Milk*, was based on that series of small tragedies.

Now that Martha is a grown woman, she spills milk less often. Nevertheless, whenever it (or grape juice, Tab, or tea) gets spilled, all family members can be depended upon to chant in bad harmony, "where two or three are gathered, someone spills the . . ." The mess is just as messy as ever, but the childhood memory, now healed, provides ointment for the irritation.

Adolescent fears and frustrations form the adult. Repressed, they can become part of the inner darkness about which Freud warned. If, however, those same fears emerge as anecdotes from childhood, they can often be resolved. Our son, Brett, has struggled through the teenage years, particularly those situations in which threats to his masculinity arose. Like countless boys, his models for "he-manliness" often came from movie stars and athletes, whose styles of dress he therefore imitated.

On one occasion Brett entered the kitchen dressed in a manner that would have made Clint Eastwood proud. His shirt was open to the waist, and he was wearing a chain with some sort of macho symbol—I think it was a razor blade—hanging from it. No one would have dared take away his gusto.

Except his sister, Martha. Glancing sideways at her brother, her eyes turned toward the ceiling and she commented to no one in particular: "O. H. O. C."

Brett, alert to Martha's blunt ways from previous encounters, was immediately attentive. "O. H. O. C.? What's that mean, Martha?"

"One-hair-on-chest!"

The reply was not well received at the time. However, the boy became a man, and he is now able to tell that incident—with certain improvements—to others. It becomes a way for dealing with some of the insecurities and embarrassments from his adolescence.

Adult memories can be healed in similar fashion. All of us have known times of rejection and disappointment that hurt like the dickens. Later, at a family reunion, these events become anecdotes. The stories are mostly true, but they are no longer tragic remembrances.

Many authors and would-be authors tell about their rejection notices from publishers. All died a little—or a lot—when they received those unwelcome words: "We regret that your manuscript does not meet our editorial needs at this time." Those of us who have received such literal words of rejection may head for bed, assume the prenatal position, and turn the electric blanket up to nine. When we recall the event later, however, it's worth a few laughs. And it's cheaper than sticking pins into voodoo dolls with the editor's name inscribed.

Humiliation is one of the personal sorrows for which humor functions as a healing agent. Sentences that begin "I was so embarrassed I could die . . ." are previews of anecdotes to come. The words offer a clue as to why humor heals humiliation: we were, indeed, embarrassed but we did not, in fact, die. Frequently, we also discover how completely private our humiliation was. Others, looking on, did not see it that way at all.

When I was a young pastor, I was asked to fly to Boston from Indiana to speak at a major gathering. The other speakers were well-known church leaders with impressive credentials. My fame was local, extending barely to the city limits. The invitation to be on the program was mostly coincidental, and I went to Boston in a state of high anxiety. I had leadings from both the Lord and my stomach that I was out of my league.

The format for the event included the introduction of all four speakers, each of whom was to make a brief statement before we went on to other business. The presiding officer, author and pastor Bruce Larson, first introduced William Stringfellow, the dynamic and controversial churchman who made his comments in typically provocative style. Next came Dr. Franklin Littell, a distinguished Methodist historian whose presence on the program had attracted a large segment of the audience. The third speaker to be introduced was Richard Halverson, a well-known evangelical Presbyterian pastor and recently chaplain of the United States Senate.

By process of elimination I was next. As the Bible directs, I girded up my loins and prepared to speak. But wait!! Bruce Larson was moving on to the next part of the program. He had forgotten I was there!!

But I was there! Fifteen hundred people sitting in the audience could see me, and my name was listed on the program. The audience noticed something was remiss, and their rustling caused Bruce to check his notes. Quickly, he apologized and said, "I'm sorry, I almost forgot to introduce our final speaker, Mr. Tim Miller."

Years later I reminded Bruce Larson of that incident. He didn't even remember it! His forgetting, however, was undoubtedly a more accurate reflection of its importance than was my humiliation. Many tellings of that story later, it's clear to me that the problem was rooted in my own insecurity and anxiety, my own lack of confidence. The memory is still part of my consciousness, but its pain is gone.

Humorous laughter can grow out of disappointment. If we expect to drive a tack in the carpet and drive in our thumb instead, we will experience pain, but the incident can eventually be funny. When we realize that our thumb healed, that we *didn't* die from embarrassment, that we *survived* adolescence, and that our children grew up *without* being arrested—then we can laugh.

That is why to this day I honestly feel no humiliation about that time in Boston, and I have nothing but respect and affection for my friend, Brice Leerson.

Resources for Discussion

1. Were you ever in a situation wherein you were laughing on the outside but crying on the inside? Can you talk about it to others now?
2. Do you agree with Elton Trueblood who says that laughter can be a natural expression of deep pain? What does he mean? Is this true to your experience?
3. Are there anecdotes about embarrassing or humiliating events from your past that delight others as you tell them now?
4. Transforming painful memories into anecdotes, says the author, enables us to remember and forgive. Is this true for you? When you remember, by way of anecdotes, persons who once caused you pain, do you recall them with resentment? Or have your memories of that teacher or playground bully or insensitive acquaintance been healed?
5. Do you agree that certain forms of humor are themselves a kind of disappointment? Does learning to laugh at jokes wherein things don't turn out right prepare us for real life disappointments? Or is this to claim too much for the healing power of humor?
6. Charlie Chaplin said: "Playful pain—that is what humor is. The minute a thing is overtragic, it is funny." Is this what happens when we translate painful experiences into funny anecdotes—we discover they are overtragic?

7. What is the difference between an event which was painful at the time it occurred and remains so today, and one which is healed by humor? Is there a need for more time and distance? For forgiving another? Is an event still painful because its tragic consequences can still be felt?

12

Families That Laugh, Last

Two couples are making conversation. One woman remarks to her female counterpart, "I said to myself just today that if food prices keep going up, I'll have to get a husband who makes more money." Later, the husband of the joke-teller comments about a wedding gift they had given to a niece. "We gave them a vacuum sweeper. It had been given to us five years ago, but it had never been used."

A wife needling her husband about being a poor provider? A husband joking about her sloppy housekeeping? Is this couple's marriage breaking apart?

Probably not. Usually, in fact, such jokes are a means of showing closeness. They indicate that neither is sensitive about such subjects. This runs contrary to the view some anthropologists hold, namely, that teasing and kidding are done to deliver messages or deliberately give offense.

This can be the case, of course, as we've already seen. Yet, when the joking and teasing stops, marriages and friendships may be on their deathbeds. This poses a significant question: If diminishing humor is a sign of a deteriorating relationship, will restoring joking and teasing provide healing?

Yes. Joking can bring a delicate topic out into the open or show concern about a problem. Solid marriages and friendships invariably include being "in fun." What is it couples long for, want to restore, that may have been missing lately? It's probably the "stuff" that goes into a relationship to make it happy —enjoying each other, laughing with one another, joking, and gentle teasing. These are as symbolic of a healthy relationship as is romance.

Because humor effectively cushions statements or "tests the water," it enables persons to express love or communicate affection without forcing the other to "get romantic." My father was representative of a generation which had difficulty in articulating words of affection or love. Dad showed his love and respect for Mother by deeds—being a good provider, living a decent life, and assuming family responsibility. He seldom, however, said "I love you" to Mother.

On one occasion I overheard Mother say to Dad, "Bert, how come you never tell me you love me any more?" Dad, though a person of few words, had an excellent sense of humor. With a twinkle he replied: "Bernice, I told you that once, and if I change my mind, I'll tell you so."

The long-standing slogan, "the family that prays together stays together," is full of truth. I would add, "the family that *plays* together"—meaning laughing, joking, and teasing—"stays together." Their chances of making it as a family unit are enhanced if there is a shared sense of fun. Parents can positively affect the tone of the family if fun and horseplay are not only allowed but encouraged. Children usually rejoice in healthy teasing and, in fact, may feel excluded if left out. Indeed, children who feel rejected often show it in one of two ways—by delinquent behavior or attempts to be funny.

A family is blessed when some among its members assume the role of Head of Horseplay. Most families depend upon certain ones to provide the life of the party, just as they look to other members for strength or responsibility. They rephrase the fifth commandment into "humor thy father and mother."

In our family the number-two daughter, Martha, has regularly assumed that role. Her view of life is built around the strategic importance of having fun. Upon returning, exhausted, from a three-day trip that included a hectic schedule and six-hundred miles of driving, I was greeted by Martha in typical fashion: "Hi, Dad, did you have fun?" It was she who at age seven put vaseline on her parents' bedroom doorknob and left artificial vomit on the porches of selected customers on her paper route when she went to collect. Years later, at the dinner honoring her and other intiates into Phi Beta Kappa, the speaker talked for one hour and thirty-three minutes on a topic fascinating to himself. At the end of the first hour, Martha forced the rest of us into painful suppression of laughter merely by writing on a napkin, "Try not to think about going to the bathroom!"

Children acquire parents when they (the parents)

are so old it is hard to change their habits. The Marthas of the world are essential to strong families because they bring a natural commitment to mischief and fun. They keep parents alert and free from complacency. Jennifer Owsley demonstrated this spirit in her essay, "A Handy Guide to Grown-ups":

> The more adults you get to know, the more you will realize each one is different. If you think they are all like your mother, you will get fooled.
>
> Adults are not just big children. They think and act differently.
>
> One of the reasons for this is that when you grow up you get larger and can reach higher places, and so you can do different things. For instance, when you were four you probably couldn't see over the edge of the kitchen sink. When you get bigger you can see right down into it. So you know what washing dishes is like. This is fun at first.
>
> If you were twice as high as you are, elevators would not frighten you because you would not have your head pressed between people's stomachs. The furniture would fit you, and it wouldn't get you anywhere to climb up on it. Probably that's why adults don't climb. Besides, they are too stiff.
>
> They think differently because they have been in this world longer and have had more time to learn about everything and get used to it. So they aren't so surprised about the world anymore.[1]

Furthermore, between the innocence of childhood and the dignity of adulthood there comes into being one of God's most complex creations—the teenager. Teenagers come in assorted sizes, weights, and colors, but they share a common creed—to keep all adults in a state of anxiety, fluctuating between high hopes for the future of the world and complete despair for all living things.

For this reason psychologists and family counselors invest inordinate time and energy in analyzing and explaining teenage behavior. Who knows how many family problems could have been avoided were homes the place where mischief and horseplay were at least accepted and possibly rewarded? Being "in fun" communicates acceptance, appreciation, and love.

When an atmosphere of good humor has been established, the manner in which discipline is administered changes. Just as couples who are able to tease one another demonstrate intimacy and equality by their joking, so is healthy teasing a way of providing criticism within a context that says life is serious but not depressing.

When it was necessary to discipline Martha as she was growing up—which wasn't easy because her sins were usually hilarious—we would say to her, "Martha, the reason we are doing this is because we don't love you as much as the other children!" Because she was loved so much she often got away with high crimes, the comment was clearly a joke. After awhile, she would anticipate that little speech, and it became one way of being firm and loving at the same time.

Many homes are devoid of laughter. Families substitute entertainment (for example, watching television or going places to see a performance) for being "in fun" together. When family members experience the process of loving one another, they

119

allow some to tease and others to laugh. And their laughter builds bridges to joy.

Marriage and family for Christians represent the essential environments for bearing burdens, witnessing to the world, and transcending pain. Anger and frustration are inherently part of the experience, as sure as taxes and more taxes. Humorous laughter reduces the tension and softens the blows. Its value is sometimes realized only when it is missing. Then it becomes conspicuous by its absence.

Martha's question for her father when he came home tired and weary after long, hard days is one that many families might consider. As we share life together, it's fair to ask, "Are we having any fun?"

Resources for Discussion

1. Recall your childhood days. Were teasing and joking a significant part of the experience? Did someone in the family assume a primary role of being the chief mischief maker? Did your parents encourage laughter?
2. In your courtship and marriage—or that of close friends—what role do teasing and joking play? Was it done to "deliver messages" or express hostility, or was it a sign that the couple enjoyed being "in fun" together?
3. The author says that many families substitute entertainment (being spectators together) for being "in fun." What is the difference? Are these direct opposites? Can entertainment, such as watching television, become a source of genuine family fun? How?
4. The exerpt from "A Handy Guide to Grownups" was written by a girl not yet eleven years old. Its point is that children look at the world with fresh eyes, almost like poets. If children, however, are supposed to add delight and freshness to a family, why are so many young adults choosing *not* to have them? In your experience, has childlikeness been a virtue?
5. Has humor been a means for reducing anger and frustration in your family? Or has it been a negative factor—for example, "Don't make jokes when I'm speaking to you, young man!"
6. The "happy family" is regarded as an American "right" or at least a privilege. Commercials con-

tinually picture adults and children in family groups laughing and joking. In this picture of family happiness, why are the people laughing? Does a product, such as Kentucky Fried Chicken, promote laughter? Can a video-game or other toy? What is Madison Avenue's understanding of being "in fun"?

13

Happy Endings

The workshop was entitled, "The Healing Power of Humor," and we were in its third session. One participant, choking back tears, shared her story:

"I came to this workshop with one question. Eight months ago my husband died and since that time I've experienced unrelenting depression. We used to have so much fun together, and now I am always sad. My question is: Will I ever laugh again?"

The group and the leader sat in silence for a moment, too moved to speak. Finally another woman responded: "I think I know how you feel. I went through a similar time four years ago myself, only it was my mother who had died. Like you, I felt totally depressed. Mother was the life of our family, and her sudden death left a terrible void. There was no group to ask it of, but I, too, wondered if we could ever again feel the same sense of fun and good times we had had.

"I can still remember the day I got an answer," she continued. "My sister and I had gone to the cemetery to plant flowers on Mother's grave. This was about five months after her death, the first opportunity the weather had given us.

"Her grave was located a long walk from a water supply. My sister and I had carried two big buckets of water with us for setting out the plants. We had placed the buckets behind us as we dug in the soil getting it ready for the flowers. In the process I managed to kick over one bucket of water, causing my sister instinctively to jump back and knock over the other one!

"We looked at each other, kneeling in a small sea of mud and water. Suddenly, my sister began to laugh. 'You know,' she said, 'I bet Mom is up there right now looking down on us, saying "you girls always did make the biggest messes the world has ever seen."'

"I laughed and my sister laughed, and we both laughed some more. The weight of our depression was lifted. Sometimes I think about Mother, and I'm still sad. But I also know I can laugh again."

That account, reconstructed from memory, has the ring of truth. It agrees with the experience of many others who have experienced loss and grief. We wonder, will we ever be happy again? And one day we laugh, and it is as if God has reminded us that sorrow does not cancel joy any more than present laughter precludes future tears.

Bernard Shaw, who claimed to be an atheist, once wrote, "Life does not cease to be funny when people die, any more than it ceases to be serious when people laugh." Those persuaded by the Christian faith go further. Laughter in, around, or in spite of grief is an affirmation that death itself is not final. Therefore, it is not ultimately serious. Leslie Weatherhead put it this way: "The opposite of joy is not sorrow. It is unbelief."

Many of us have attended funerals which were a witness to this affirmation. Persons whose lives had demonstrated both a serious commitment to Christ as well as the quality of being "in fun" were remembered at their deaths with tears *and* laughter. An excellent example of this combination is seen in the tribute Gerald Kennedy offered to his friend, Halford Luccock, shortly after Luccock's death. Bishop Kennedy wrote:

> The last few years of his life found me the lucky participant in a three-way correspondence with Dr. Luccock and Emory Burke. . . . The letters were always marked *Personal* because they were utterly frank, and they were better than an hour on the analyst's couch. Hal spoke his mind about Yale lectures, publishers, bishops, and church machinery. He commented on contemporary trends which displeased him, and now and then he would explode. It was wonderful. His typing was so bad that I could hardly make it out, and I told him once that he was the only friend I ever had whose letters were hardly legible even when typewritten.
>
> Now those letters have stopped coming, and I miss them more than I know how to say. It always lifted up my heart to know that Halford Luccock was around somewhere. *Gradually it has come to me that he is still around somewhere, and I am comforted*[1] [Italics mine].

Bishop Kennedy, in speaking of his friend in a serious but light-hearted way, illustrates a key insight about humor. Humorous laughter can be a theological affirmation, a testimony to God's trustworthiness. "Gradually it has come to me that he is still around somewhere, and I am comforted."

Peter Berger elaborates on this point. "From the Christian point of view one can say that comedy, unlike tragedy, bears within it a great secret. This secret is the promise of redemption. For redemption promises in eternity what comedy gives us in its few moments of precarious liberation—the collapse of the walls of our imprisonment."[2] The Reaper is grim because the joke is on him.

It was an ancient custom in Greek Orthodox circles to set aside the day after Easter as a day of laughter and hilarity. As Conrad Hyers makes clear, that particular celebration treated "joking and jesting [as] appropriate within the sanctuary because of the big joke God pulled on Satan in the Resurrection. Cosmos has been victorious over chaos, faith over doubt, trust over anxiety; and humanity is now truly free to laugh with the laughter of higher innocence."[3]

A sense of humor combined with faith helps us grasp the Big Picture. A comic view of life, even as death nears, allows room for laughter, and laughter nourishes our daily existence. If we can laugh in the face of death, then we certainly can enjoy funny things on the way to the cemetery.

The Big Picture affects the way we view humanity as we make that trip. Peter Berger, once again, helps us see this: "There is always an awareness that this particular colossus staring us in the face at the moment, like all the colossi of this world, is swallowed up in Christ's victory and will be swept away when this victory is consummated. Nothing human is ultimately dangerous, not even the most determined stupidity. Thus nothing human can ultimately keep us from the liberation of laughter."[4]

Appropriately, an old joke from World War II captures the essence of Berger's point. It seems Hitler, Stalin, and Churchill were called together by God and told that victory would be granted to the first one able to drain the Atlantic Ocean. That would prove which nation was on the side of justice. Hitler and Stalin protested loudly that the task was unfair and refused to participate. Churchill, on the other hand, took a small bucket and began scooping water from the ocean. "It may take a long, long time," he said, "but we're going to win this war."

If life is ultimately tragic, our laughter at best is simply escapist and, at worst, bitter and cynical. If, as the Christian faith affirms, God's ultimate purposes eventually will prevail, the story has a happy ending.

In the workshop which was mentioned earlier, the group did an exercise which examined the idea that humor is evidence of God's faithfulness. Participants were asked to compose in one or two sentences an epitaph for themselves which would capture the way they wanted to be remembered.

Most of the "epitaphs" were predictable. They were modest or serious or bland: "She did what she could with what she had." "He shared his life and faith and had plenty left over for himself."

One man, however, was more profound than he knew in the words of his epitaph. We read our creations aloud, and his happened to come last. What he wanted written on his tombstone, he said, were these words: "I'd rather be home in bed with my wife."

That was a tribute to his wife—and, in a way, to his faith. We choose life but death is a reality. A life of faith, however, allows room to laugh in the face of tragedy. But, shucks, that's not news. Jesus already said so: "In the world you have tribulation; but be of good cheer, I have overcome the world." (John 16:33, RSV)

Life has a happy ending. Let us rejoice and be glad.

Resources for Discussion

1. A surprising number of persons have had funny experiences that were associated with tragic situations. One woman told of taking a hot-air balloon ride and asking to land by her parents' grave. Her comment: "I just can't think of a better way to visit. They would love it if they could know!" Have you experienced similar combinations of laughter and grief?

2. Some Christian writers differentiate between *humorous laughter* and *joy*. Joy refers to a sense of exultation that comes out of a faithful, trusting relationship with Christ. Humorous laughter, on the other hand, suggests the natural enjoyment we get from the incongruities and ironies of life. This author connects the two. An ability to laugh at the stuff of life while simultaneously experiencing grief witnesses to God's trustworthiness. Do you agree? Can humorous laughter be an affirmation of faith?

3. Consider Peter Berger's comment: "Nothing human is ultimately dangerous, not even the most determined stupidity. Thus nothing human can ultimately keep us from the liberation of laughter." What does he mean? What does faith in Christ have to do with this?

4. Play the epitaph game the author describes. In a sentence or two write your own epitaph. What place has laughter held in your lifelong trip to the cemetery?

5. Reinhold Niebuhr says that a "sense of humor remains healthy only when it deals with *immediate* issues—It must move toward faith or sink in despair when the ultimate issues are raised." This seems to argue against seeing humorous laughter as an act of faith. Has laughter been totally missing from your experiences of facing ultimate issues?

NOTES

Chapter 1

1. William H. Martineau, "A Model of the Social Functions of Humor," *The Psychology of Humor,* ed. Jeffrey H. Goldstein and Paul E. McGhee (New York: Academic Press, 1972), p. 111.

2. See Sigmund Freud, *The Complete Psychological Works: Standard Edition,* ed. and trans. James Strachey (New York: W. W. Norton, 1976), vol. 8, *Jokes and Their Relation to the Unconscious.*

Chapter 2

1. Max Eastman, *Enjoyment of Laughter* (New York: Simon & Schuster, 1936), p. 3.

2. Arthur Guiterman, *Lyric Laughter* (New York: E. P. Dutton, 1939), p. 39.

3. Gelett Burgess, *The Burgess Nonsense Book* (New York: Frederick Stokes, 1901), p. 24.

4. Ogden Nash, *Family Reunion* (Boston: Little, Brown, & Co., 1950), p. 71.

Chapter 3

1. Reinhold Niebuhr, *Discerning the Signs of the Times* (New York: Charles Scribner's Sons, 1946), p. 122.

2. St. Ambrose, quoted in Hugo Rahner, *Eutrapelia: A Forgotten Virtue,* in *Holy Laughter,* ed. Conrad Hyers (New York: Seabury Press, 1969).

3. Robert Barclay, "Proposition XV: Concerning Salutations and Recreations, Etc.," *Apology for the True Christian Divinity,* 19th ed. (London: Harvey and Dalton, 1841), p. 488.

4. Chad Walsh, "On Being With It: An Afterword," in *Holy Laughter,* p. 242.

5. Raymond Moody, *Laugh After Laugh* (Jacksonville, Fl.: Headwaters Press, 1978), p. 82.

6. Conrad Hyers, "The Dialectic of the Sacred and the Comic," in *Holy Laughter,* p. 212.

Chapter 4

1. Ruth W. Washburn, "A Study of Smiling and Laughing of Infants in the First Year of Life," *Genetic Psychology Monographs,* no. IV, 1929, pp. 297–337.

2. Clifton Fadiman, "Humor as a Weapon," *The Center Magazine,* January-February 1971, p. 22.

Chapter 5

1. Reinhold Niebuhr, *Discerning the Signs of the Times* (New York: Charles Scribner's Sons, 1946), pp. 119f.

Chapter 6

1. Mark Twain, "The War Prayer," from Mark Twain, *The War Prayer* (New York: St. Crispin Press, copyright 1923, 1951 by The Mark Twain Company).

2. Conrad Hyers, "The Dialectic of the Sacred and the Comic," in *Holy Laughter* (New York: Seabury Press, 1969), p. 208.

Chapter 7

1.Ben Patterson, "Dirty Jokes" (editorial), *The Wittenburg Door,* April-May 1981, p. 3.

Chapter 8

1. Chris Mullins, "The Senator's Little Joke Was Not Kind of Funny," *Kansas City Times,* 6 March 1980.

2. J. N. Burma, "Humor As a Technique in Race Conflict," *American Sociological Review,* 1946, pp. 710–715.

Chapter 10
1. See *The Saturday Review,* 28 May 1977, pp. 4f.
2. Raymond A. Moody, Jr., *Laugh After Laugh* (Jacksonville, Fl.: Headwaters Press, 1978), p. 82.

Chapter 11
1. Raymond A. Moody, Jr., *Laugh After Laugh* (Jacksonville, Fl.: Headwaters Press, 1978), pp. 87–88.
2. Elton Trueblood, *The Humor of Christ* (New York: Harper & Row, 1964), p. 23.

Chapter 12
1. Jennifer Owsley, "A Handy Guide to Grown-Ups," *The Reader's Digest Treasury of American Humor* (New York: American Heritage Press, 1972), p. 560.

Chapter 13
1. Gerald H. Kennedy, "Introduction," *Halford Luccock Treasury,* ed. Robert E. Luccock (Nashville: Abingdon Press, 1963), pp. 8f.
2. Peter Berger, *The Precarious Vision* (Garden City: New York, Doubleday, 1961), p. 214.
3. Conrad Hyers, "The Dialectic of the Sacred and the Comic," in *Holy Laughter* (New York: Seabury Press, 1969), p. 239.
4. Berger, *The Precarious Vision,* p. 215.